Better Billiards and Snooker

£1-50

Clive Everton

BETTER BILLIARDS
AND SNOOKER

Table diagrams by Peter F. Chaplin

KAYE & WARD · LONDON

First published in Great Britain by
Kaye & Ward Ltd
The Windmill Press
Kingswood, Tadworth, Surrey
1975
Revised Edition 1981
Copyright © Kaye & Ward Ltd 1975
Paperback edition first published 1985

ISBN 0 7182 1480 3

Printed and bound in Great Britain by
Biddles Ltd, Guildford and King's Lynn

Contents

Basic Rules

BILLIARDS

The game of billiards is played with three balls: two whites and a red. The game starts with the red on the spot (diagram 1). Players spin a coin or 'string' for the choice of playing first or for the choice of the two white balls. One of these balls has two small black spots and is referred to as 'spot', while the other is called 'plain'.

The first player may place his ball anywhere within the D for his first shot.

The first player must play the red with his first shot. If his white drives the red into a pocket (pot red) or if his white enters a pocket after contacting the red (in-off red), he scores 3. If, on the other hand, he misses the red (a miss), his opponent scores 1. If he misses the red and the white enters a pocket (a coup), his opponent scores 3.

When the first player fails to score, the second player places his ball anywhere within the D and may play at either the red or at his opponent's white, provided the latter is not in baulk (the area between the baulk line and the baulk cushion).

In addition to the methods of scoring outlined above, when there are only two balls on the table the second player may drive his opponent's white into a pocket (pot white), cause his own white to enter a pocket after striking his opponent's white (in-off white) or cause his own white to strike both the red and his opponent's white (cannon). Each of these scoring shots is valued at 2 points.

The game then proceeds with players taking alternate turns (or innings) until one of them reaches a pre-arranged points target (e.g. 100 or 1000 points), although in championships players play a variable number of two-hour sessions.

1

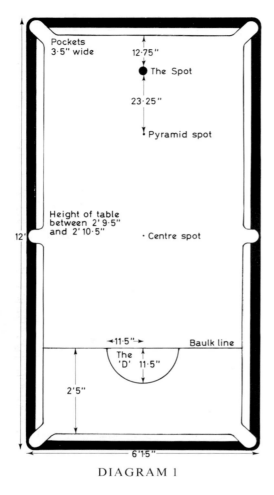

Pockets
3·5" wide

12·75"

The Spot

23·25"

Pyramid spot

Height of table
between 2'9·5"
and 2'10·5"

Centre spot

12'

11·5"

Baulk line

The
'D' 11·5"

2'5"

6'15"

DIAGRAM 1

Each time a player scores an in-off, his ball is returned to him to place anywhere within the D for his next shot. This is known as 'playing from hand'. When doing this, the player's own ball (cue-ball) must initially leave baulk before striking another ball.

Each time the red is potted it is returned to its own spot. When this is occupied by another ball, it is placed on the pyramid spot. If a player pots the red from its spot five times in succession it is then placed on the middle spot until it is potted again. If a player pots his opponent's white, this remains in the pocket until it is his opponent's turn to play. On any occasion when a player fails to contact an object-ball (except when the striker is in hand and there is no ball out of baulk) his opponent, in addition to any penalties incurred, has the option of playing from the position left or having the balls spotted – red on its own spot, opponent's white on the middle spot and cue-ball in hand.

Players of an advanced standard have to watch for the '15 hazards' rule (a hazard is an archaic term for a pot or in-off). The rule limits a player to fifteen consecutive pots and/or in-offs. To continue his break, he must play a cannon at least once every sixteen shots. The referee 'warns' a player after ten hazards. A player is limited to seventy-five consecutive cannons but, since there are less than half a dozen players capable of maintaining such a lengthy sequence, this rule rarely needs to be applied.

2

SNOOKER

Snooker is played with twenty-two coloured balls, which are positioned at the start of a game (or frame) as shown in diagram 2. The cue-ball, which is used alternately by both players, can be placed anywhere in the D for the first stroke, but must thereafter be played from where it comes to rest.

Points are scored by potting and by penalties. Each player must first attempt to strike a red (value 1). When he pots a red he must then play at a colour. The colours carry different values: black 7, pink 6, blue 5, brown 4, green 3, yellow 2. The player must nominate the colour he is attempting, although, when this is obvious, observance of the letter of this rule is invariably waived. If a colour is potted, it is replaced on its own spot and another red is then attempted, and so on until all the reds have been potted. The colours are then taken

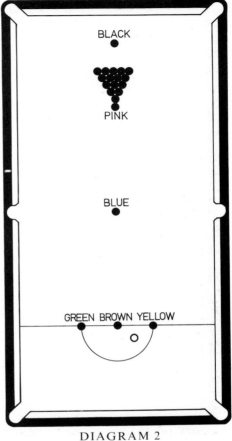

DIAGRAM 2

in ascending order of value, until only the cue-ball remains on the table. Skilful players can often compile a sequence of pots, which is known as a 'break'.

Failure to strike a red involves a penalty of 4 points (the minimum penalty for any foul), but the penalty is increased to 5, 6 or 7 if, instead of a red, the cue-ball strikes blue, pink or black. An in-off is a foul carrying a penalty of 4 points, or more if the ball which the cue-ball strikes before entering a pocket is of higher value. After an in-off, the next player may place the cue-ball anywhere within the D. Failure to strike a nominated

3

colour also carries a 4 point penalty, or more if the ball involved is of higher value. If, for example, brown is nominated but black is struck, the penalty is 7. If black is nominated and green is struck, the penalty is also 7.

Most points are scored by potting, but penalties are often the result not of inadvertency or chance but of skilfully laid snookers. A snooker occurs when the balls are so placed that a player cannot strike the ball he is due to play without first hitting a cushion or making the cue-ball swerve. The snooker very often has a tactical importance beyond the acquisition of a 4–7 point penalty.

If a player is snookered on the reds after a foul shot by his opponent, he may nominate any coloured ball as a red. This is known as a 'free ball'. If he pots it, he scores 1 and can then nominate a colour in the usual way. If no red remains, a free ball is valued at the same number of points as the lowest valued colour remaining and the colours are then taken in sequence. For the purpose of this rule, a player is deemed to be snookered if he cannot directly hit both extremities of the object-ball.

FOUL SHOTS

After any foul shot, whether he is entitled to a free ball or not, a player can ask his opponent to play again. A foul is committed in both billiards and snooker if:

(a) a player's cue-tip strikes the cue-ball more than once in the same stroke
(b) if a ball is forced off the table
(c) if a player plays with both feet off the floor
(d) if a player plays before all the balls have come to rest
(e) if a player strikes or touches a ball other than with the tip of the cue
(f) by causing the cue-ball to jump over any other ball
(g) by playing with the balls wrongly spotted.

If at the end of a frame the scores are level, the black is replaced on its spot and the player winning the toss of a coin has the choice of whether he or his opponent takes first shot at it from anywhere within the D.

4

Grip, Stance and Striking

GRIP AND STANCE

It is easy to grip the cue correctly. Just pick it up at the thick end (the butt) as if you were going to hit someone over the head with it. Then, assuming you are right-handed, stand sideways to the table like a batsman, a golfer, a boxer or a tennis-player about to serve. Place the thin end of

1. The cue should be picked up as if you are about to hit someone over the head with it. It should be held with just enough strength to keep it horizontal when it has no other support. A grip that is too loose will not allow you to have complete control of the cue, and a grip that is too tight will produce tension in the muscles of the forearm, which will lead to loss of fluency as you play your shot. If the match situation produces tension, which makes you grip the cue too tightly, make a conscious effort to relax.

2. This side view of Willie Thorne illustrates a number of important straight lines in a player's stance: the right rear leg is braced and straight; the lower arm is perpendicular from elbow to wrist; the cue is running as near horizontally as the table allows it. The front leg is bent, with the foot pointing in the direction of the shot. The player's weight should be on the bent front leg, with the back leg straight.

the cue between the thumb and first finger of your left hand, and draw it across your body at waist height, like an archer stretching a bow. Then, bending the left leg but keeping the right leg straight, lower the left hand on to the table. Spread the fingers wide apart, gripping the cloth firmly, and cock the thumb.

You should now be in possession of a basically sound grip, stance and bridge, though each player tends to make his own small adjustments in order to feel comfortable. The left foot should be pointing almost on the same line as the cue. The right foot sometimes strays round to bring the player more chest-on to the shot, but it is a mistake to allow the foot

6

to stray too much. Indeed, 'stand sideways on' seems to be a sound principle in most sports.

You will notice that photograph 2 shows the player's weight on the bent leading leg with the back leg ramrod straight. This rock steady stance is essential because, as the cue travels through to make the shot, the only part of the body which should move is the right arm from the elbow downwards. Sometimes, on forcing shots, there is some movement from the right shoulder (which is why forcing shots tend to be missed more than medium or medium-fast shots), but concentrate on keeping this to a minimum.

ALIGNING THE SHOT

On the shot, the cue should lightly brush the chin directly beneath your nose so that you can concentrate both eyes equally on your shot. Billiards and snooker are games in which minute fractions often matter a great deal, so if you 'favour' one eye at the expense of the other, by having the cue run underneath one eye rather than between them, the perspective of the shot can be distorted just enough to spoil the shot. Having said this, however, a number of good players (including Willie Thorne, who had not realized it until these pictures were taken) have their cues running beneath their left eye. Rex Williams, the World Professional Billiards' Champion, is a notable example of this and the great Joe Davis, whose right eye was weak, was the most notable of all. The fact remains that, while this slight eccentricity suits some players, the vast majority are better off running the cue under their nose.

Most professionals have this perfect or near-perfect alignment between elbow, cue and eye but again there are exceptions. Ray Reardon, six times World Professional Snooker Champion, who broke his shoulder when he was a boy, plays with his right elbow jutting out. This inevitably means that his wrist is turned outwards. If you have as much natural ability as he does there is nothing to worry about, but most players function more effectively if the line from elbow to wrist is perpendicular, which it cannot be if the elbow is turned out.

The side view of the stance (photograph 5, p. 10) shows how the cue arm should act as a hinge. If the cue arm is perpendicular there is no impediment

7

to a full backswing, but many beginners make the mistake of holding the cue too far back, so that they can swing forward but cannot swing very far back. This inevitably produces a jerky action, which is all against good play.

These are the main *principles* of stance you should observe. I stress *principles* because we are all slightly different in our physical make-up. Try to make your technique more sound, but do not make it stereotyped – evolve your own style, based on sound general principles, rather than try to make yourself a carbon copy of a player you admire.

THE BRIDGE

The fingers of your left hand should be widely spread on the table and the thumb cocked. Bring the forefinger up to the thumb to make a narrow channel through which the cue can comfortably travel without deviating from a straight course. If this channel is too wide, you will find it impossible to prevent the cue wobbling from side to side as you make your shot.

3. The standard bridge shows the thumb cocked and the fingers widely spread with the forefinger at an angle which gives the cue extra support as it runs between the channel formed by the thumb and the top knuckle of the first finger. The fingers are gripping the cloth to provide stability and the cue is running horizontally as it addresses the cue-ball.

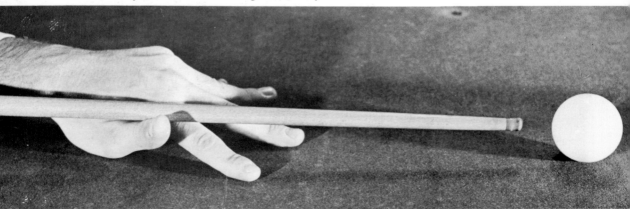

4. The chin should lightly brush the cue, so that the player is looking as nearly as possible along the line of the shot. Most good players sight with the cue on the chin directly between the eyes, but some sight by bringing their cues more beneath one eye – usually the left. The most extreme example of this is Graham Miles, twice Pot Black champion, whose cue runs almost underneath his left ear, but this individual style has been developed through a number of experiments over several years. In fact, in Miles's amateur days, he sighted directly between the eyes.

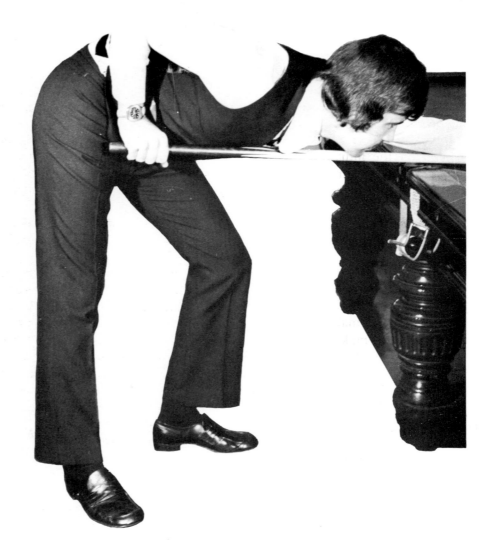

5. The back arm should be perpendicular from elbow to wrist so that it can act as a hinge and will not impede either a full backswing or a full follow through.

STRIKING THE CUE-BALL

You are now equipped to strike the cue-ball. Accuracy in this department is one of the most underestimated but most important parts of the game.

You should place your bridge hand about 9″ from the cue-ball, with your cue addressing it plumb centre. Try this and see how comfortable you feel. Is your rear leg far enough back? Or are you humped up, so that your eyes are not looking nearly horizontally but at an angle into the bed of the table?

Is your left arm bent or straight? This is a question which really does depend on the individual: Joe Davis pushed his left arm out absolutely straight, whereas three times World Champion John Spencer plays with his arm bent. Experiment until you find which is most comfortable, but remember that it is good to get as low on your shot as possible.

When you are feeling comfortable, make a few preliminary addresses at the cue-ball. Is the cue moving back and forth in a straight line or is it going across the ball (i.e. from right to left or left to right)?

Novices should try as soon as possible to develop the habit of rhythmic cueing. If you go into a snooker room, you will generally see an extraordinary variety of cue actions, from first-time strikers, who seem to sneak up on the cue-ball and make a lightning, if jerky, assault without any preparation, to players who make innumerable preliminary addresses even on the easiest shots. Occasionally there is a genius who plays and sights first time – the great Frank Edwards, who won the English billiards title five times, and the dashing Indian, Satish Mohan, are obvious examples – but in general the best results are obtained by the players who make some half a dozen preliminary addresses at a steady, even tempo, building up their concentration and steadying themselves for the shot, before actually playing it.

The final backswing is important. The cue should not be taken back too fast, as there will inevitably be a jerk when it reaches the end of the backswing. Ideally the cue should go back smoothly, hesitate for a fraction of a second at the end of the backswing, and then come through clean and straight.

The picture sequence (photographs 8, 9 and 10) shows the amount of backswing and the amount of follow through appropriate to a medium-strength shot. When you have satisfied yourself that your action is reasonably

11

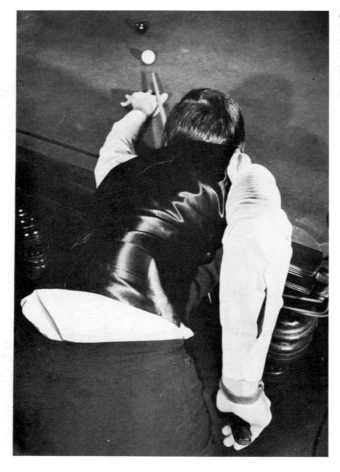

6. Though slightly distorted by the camera angle, this back view of Willie Thorne shows that his back arm is perpendicular from elbow to wrist. The point of his elbow is in fact directly behind the cue.

straight, place the cue-ball on the brown spot and play 'over the spots' to the top cushion, and back again. You should not have the slightest difficulty in sending the cue-ball up to the top cushion in a straight line, but do not be surprised if at first the cue-ball starts to return either to the left or right of the spots. This is caused by not hitting the cue-ball plumb centre, as intended, but off centre, thus unintentionally imparting some spin. If you strike the cue-ball to the right of centre (this is called 'right-hand side'), it will spin to the right on its axis, but will not, until

12

7. Willie Thorne's bridge shows the fingers widely spread for balance and maximum support. The forefinger is at an angle that gives additional support to the cue as it runs through the channel made by the part of the hand between the thumb and the top of the forefinger.

it strikes the top cushion, deviate much from its straight course. When it does strike the cushion, however, the spin will 'bite' so that the ball will run away at an angle.

The further off centre the cue-ball is struck, the wider the angle off the cushion will be (see diagram 3), though of course there does come a point when an attempt to strike too far off centre results in a mis-cue. More advanced players can, of course, adopt this use of side (side spin) to their own advantage, as we shall see later, but for the time being you should concentrate on shooting over the spots as straight as possible – first slowly, then at medium speed and finally at speed.

In general, the harder you hit the cue-ball, the more difficult it is to control it. You will find some professionals who still practise shots over

8, 9, 10. This sequence shows the cue at the furthest point of its backswing (8), just before the tip contacts the cue-ball (9), and at the furthest point of its follow-through (10). Note that the cue remains horizontal to the bed of the table throughout. (The red ball is shown only so that the distances are easier to gauge.)

14

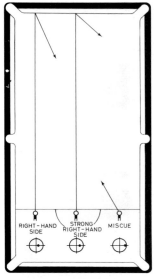

DIAGRAM 3

the spots at speed, because on forcing shots a tiny degree of unintentional side tends to be magnified in effect. One of the most common faults in forcing shots is to try to generate power from the shoulder as well as from the elbow. This inevitably means that the elbow is thrown out of alignment and the cue does not go through straight.

Once your stance is correct and comfortable, and you can shoot over the spots and back again with reasonable accuracy, you can think of trying a few game situations or a few practice games, preferably with a sympathetic and more experienced opponent.

I was lucky enough to play billiards before I played snooker. I say 'lucky' because a grounding in billiards enables one to appreciate certain aspects of snooker more quickly than if one plays only snooker. Billiards provides an all-round knowledge of ball contacts and cushion angles to such an extent that a good billiards player can always give a good account of himself at snooker, while the reverse is not necessarily true. For a variety of reasons, snooker is by far the more popular game but billiards still has a substantial number of devotees and, if recent standards in the Boys (Under 16) Championships are anything to go by, billiards could be due for at least a partial revival. The next couple of chapters are, therefore, devoted to some of the basic billiards scoring methods and moves which, if mastered, will prove useful to any player, even if he ultimately decides to concentrate solely on snooker.

Billiards: In-offs, Pots and Cannons

There are three methods (excluding penalties) by which a player scores at billiards: in-offs, pots and cannons.

IN-OFFS

The foundation of billiards is in-offs. Indeed, many players have reached amateur championship standard with a good command of in-offs and very little else. One advantage of the in-off game is that whenever you play from hand you can select the best position for the cue-ball, instead of being limited by the particular position of the balls.

Diagram 4, shot 1, shows the most basic and most valuable in-off in the game: the half-ball in-off into the middle pocket. The angle at which the cue-ball has to strike the red is an easy one for the eye to select, so, even for fairly inexperienced players, there should be little problem about the shot itself. The next step is to try to play the shot with just enough strength for the red to travel up the table, bounce off the top cushion and return to almost the same place.

Using the game's most elementary shot, we are already involved in the essence of good billiards – positional play. Positional play is based on the habit of thinking one or two shots ahead, or even in groups of shots. Obviously anything very complex is beyond the reach of the novice, but the standard 'in-off the red and bring it back' is well within anyone's capabilities with a little practice.

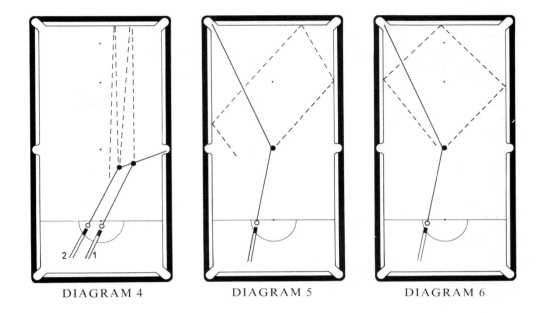

DIAGRAM 4   DIAGRAM 5   DIAGRAM 6

In the 1920s the great Australian, George Gray, made many breaks of over 1000 through this shot alone. This was as boring to watch as it was effective and led to a limitation of consecutive 'hazards' (a term embracing both pots and in-offs) to eliminate this monotonous element in the game. This limit has varied over the years and now stands at fifteen. A player is warned by the referee after he has made ten consecutive hazards. After the fifteenth hazard, a player must play a cannon to continue his break. However, the '15 limit' should not trouble novices until they have been playing for a year or two.

Diagram 4, shot 2, shows that the red has returned to almost, but not exactly, the same spot in which it was for the previous shot. To preserve the same half-ball angle it is necessary to move the cue-ball slightly further to the left than for the first shot.

As long as you can keep bringing the red back into the same area, you should continue to score quite easily, but there will be times when the red comes back either too far or not far enough. When the red does not come back far enough, you will have to play a long in-off, i.e. an in-off

17

into one of the top pockets. This is harder than the standard middle pocket in-off, but it can be mastered through practice and recognition of the required angle to the extent that the shot is rarely missed. The first long in-off to master is with the red on the middle spot. Place the cue-ball a couple of inches inside the end spot, as shown in diagram 5, and strike the red half-ball. Not only should the cue-ball disappear sweetly into the top pocket, but also the red should travel round the table off three cushions to offer a simple middle pocket in-off for your next shot.

For complete beginners it is satisfying enough simply to execute the in-off successfully; however, you will soon realise that it is profitless to play 'one-shot-at-a-time' billiards.

If you are having difficulty with this shot, it may be that you are contacting the red very slightly less than half-ball (sometimes referred to as a 'thin half-ball'), whereas, if anything, the red needs to be struck 'thick half-ball' (slightly more than half-ball). The reason for this can be seen from diagram 6, where the in-off has been played 'thin' half-ball. The red has sliced on to the right-hand side cushion, so that it strikes the left-hand side cushion almost opposite the pink spot, rather than about 9″ short of the middle pocket. On some occasions the red will remain out of position for the next in-off or, at best, will come only far enough for another long in-off, instead of the much simpler in-off in the middle.

The only way to get the 'feel' of these shots is by constant practice. Some of the outstanding billiards players practise 'red ball play' – sequences of in-offs – by the hour. However, most good players find that shorter periods of practice, provided they are regular, pay dividends.

The in-off red from the centre spot can be used as a reference point for other in-offs from that area. Start by placing the red a few inches to the right of the centre spot and then try it to the left; also try placing it a little to the left and above the centre spot, and a little to the right and below the centre spot. As you vary the position you will begin to encounter certain problems. It may be that in some positions your thick half-ball shot is merely going to bring the red ball round into the middle pocket, giving you 6 points for the shot instead of 3, but effectively ending your break.

Diagram 7 shows what may happen if you try to bring the red round, off three cushions, in the usual way. Diagrams 8 and 9 show two ways

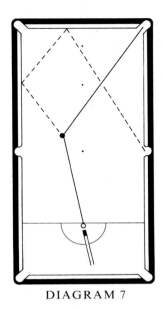

DIAGRAM 7

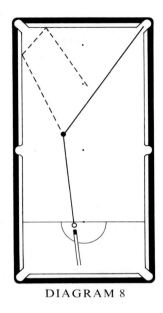

DIAGRAM 8

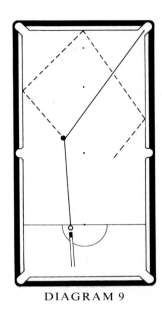

DIAGRAM 9

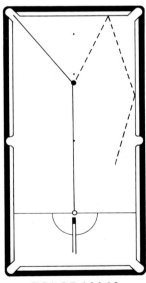

DIAGRAM 10

of avoiding this. In diagram 8, the in-off is played quite slowly, with just enough speed to bring the cue-ball off two cushions into the neighbourhood of the pink spot. In diagram 9, the in-off is played much more sharply as a thin half-ball – the very thing you were advised to avoid when playing the in-off red on the centre spot. However, a precise position alters general principles and proves that even a relatively straightforward branch of the game like red ball play has its pitfalls.

The position in which the red finished in diagram 8 leads us to another recurring type of in-off: the Y in-off. A glance at diagram 10 shows the obvious derivation of this term.

19

POTS

Potting is not, of course, as important in billiards as it is in snooker, where it is impossible to get very far without being a fairly good potter. It is broadly true to say that in billiards it is more important not to miss easy pots than to have the ability to sink spectacular long-distance pots.

The art of billiards is to control the balls in such a way that one easy shot leads to another. Ideally, one tries to do this with snooker as well, but in snooker one is very much more dependent on the precise position of the balls.

Some billiards players try to eliminate potting from their games as much as possible, but there are certain types of pot which recur constantly and must be mastered. The most notable of these is the pot red from the spot. The great players of the past realised this to such an extent that big breaks were made purely by potting reds from the spot, just as George Gray made big breaks simply from going in-off in the middle pocket. These breaks, compiled by the so-called spot stroke, led to a limitation of the number of consecutive pots which could be made from the spot. At one time the limit was as low as two but now stands at three. After five consecutive pot reds from the spot, the red is placed on the centre spot, but is placed on its own spot when it is potted again. The 15 hazards rule (i.e. one must play a cannon every sixteen shots) still applies of course.

The best way to master potting the red off its spot is to place the cue-ball for a half-ball pot on the red and see how long you can keep a spot stroke break going (see diagram 11).

As we have not yet started to discuss any of the spins which may be used for controlling the cue-ball, five pots in succession by straightforward plain ball would be quite an achievement for any novice. We will return to this later (see page 23).

CANNONS

Just as the rules had to be changed to limit the long sequences of in-offs and pots, so they also had to be amended to eliminate long runs of cannons.

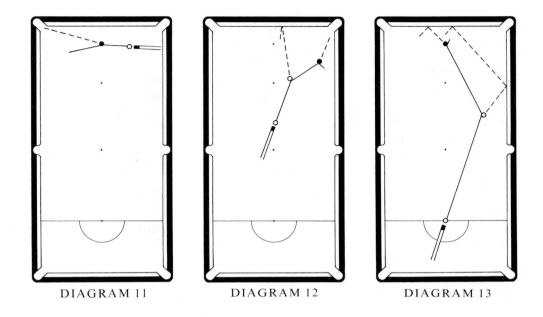

DIAGRAM 11   DIAGRAM 12   DIAGRAM 13

Using the freak 'anchor cannon' (when the red and object-white were suspended on the upper and lower jaws of the top pocket) Tom Reece made one break of 499,135. This took him three weeks and caused the anchor cannon to be outlawed. Much later, the Australian Walter Lindrum, by common consent the greatest billiards player in the history of the game, was the most notable of a group of players who mastered close cannons, which are sometimes referred to as 'nursery cannons' because the three balls are 'nursed' gently along the cushion with a series of soft, delicate cannons.

These sequences required very high degrees of skill and after a while were deadly dull to watch. Accordingly, a limit was set of thirty-five consecutive ball-to-ball cannons, which was raised to seventy-five in 1971. This rule is likely to cause trouble to less than a dozen players in the world. For everybody else the cannon is a constructive linking shot, rather than a prolonged means of scoring.

Diagram 12 shows a typical constructive cannon from object-white to red, making contact gently with the red to send it over the top pocket, so that it can be potted with the next shot. It is difficult to go very far wrong with this shot, but it is worth noticing the final position of the object-white in this shot (i.e. within a few inches of the red spot). This is an excellent place for the object-white to be, because, once the red has been potted, the two balls are obviously sufficiently close together for another cannon to help continue the break.

Good players are always looking for a chance to place the object-white near the spot, particularly with the shot shown in diagram 13, the standard 'drop cannon'. The idea here is to play from the inside of the object-white to the inside of the red in order to leave all three balls at the top of the table.

Side, Screw and Stun

Once the mechanics of grip, stance and plain ball-striking have been mastered, there are certain basic skills which have to be acquired: side, screw and stun.

SIDE

Side is imparted by the tip of the cue striking either to the left or right of the centre of the cue-ball.

Diagram 14 shows what happens when right-hand side is used. First the cue-ball pushes out slightly to the left and then curls back with the spin. When the ball strikes a cushion, the spin is fully activated so that it rebounds sharply to the right. Because of the scale of the diagram, this curve has been exaggerated.

Diagram 15 shows a simple use of side in billiards. With an ordinary plain-ball shot, the cannon is not on; by using right-hand side, however, you can not only get the shot but can also leave a good position.

Diagram 16 shows how the ball spins differently when it is travelling down the table (i.e. towards baulk). Because the ball is running against the nap of the cloth, the initial thrust to the left, which occurs when right-hand side is imparted, is maintained instead of the ball spinning to the right, though of course the ball still spins to the right after hitting a cushion.

The number of cases in which side (right-hand or left-hand) may be used is infinitely varied, but for the purposes of definition you should know the difference between 'running side' and 'check side'.

Running side is the type of side spin used in diagram 15: right-hand side has been used to widen the angle at which the cue-ball leaves the cushion and has also, incidentally, increased the distance the cue-ball will run.

23

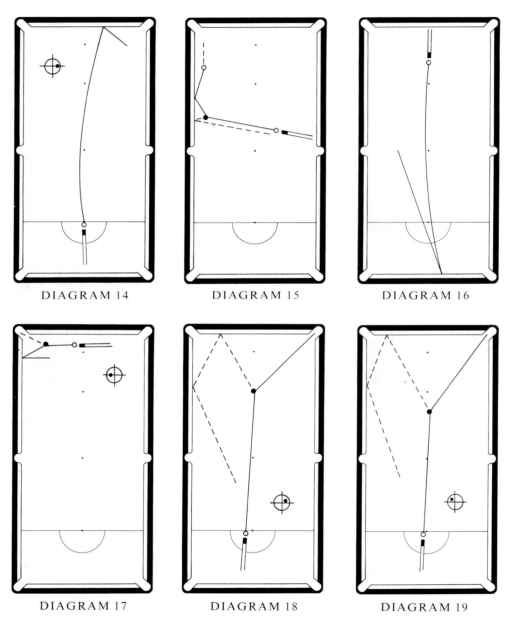

DIAGRAM 14   DIAGRAM 15   DIAGRAM 16

DIAGRAM 17   DIAGRAM 18   DIAGRAM 19

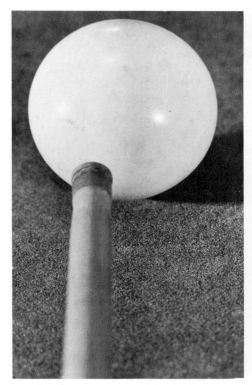

11, 12. *Never* place your bridge hand so that the tip is striking the centre of the cue-ball and then point the tip at one or other side. If you find, after you have adopted your stance for the shot, that you need to use side spin, take a new stance and bridge so that you can hit straight through the cue-ball instead of across it. Photograph 11 shows left-hand side being applied and photograph 12 shows right-hand side. (As the pictures were taken from above, it seems as if the tip is striking below centre, but in fact this is not so.)

Check side (diagram 17) does the opposite: right-hand side narrows the angle at which the cue-ball leaves the cushion and reduces the run of the cue-ball.

How can right-hand side be 'running' in one position and 'check' in another? In diagram 15 the cue-ball contacts the right of the object-ball and then, of course, the cue-ball goes to the right with the right-hand side acting as 'running' side, because it exaggerates this natural tendency. In

25

diagram 17 the cue-ball contacts the left of the object-ball and, of course, still goes to the left, but the right-hand side on the cue-ball is, as it were, fighting this natural tendency, hence the term 'check'.

There is one very important aspect of cueing to remember when using side of any description: the cue should go *through* the cue-ball rather than catch it a glancing blow. In other words, *do not* address the cue-ball in the centre and *then* hit it on one side or another, but address it at the point you intend to hit and hit straight through it.

Running and check side can also operate off balls as well as off cushions, though the effect is not as pronounced. Diagram 18 is a variant of the Y in-off. Played as a natural half ball, the red may well finish out of position, either just short of the middle pocket or just past it on the side cushion. The solution is to spot the cue-ball in the D wider than for the natural angle and play it firmly as a half-ball shot, with strong running (right-hand) side. This will throw the red off the top and side cushions, and will bring it into the middle of the table (as shown) with a much greater margin of error.

In diagram 19, a plain half-ball in-off will produce a 6-shot of a species sometimes known as a 'trouser leg'. Avoid this by spotting slightly narrower and using check (left-hand) side.

SCREW

Most novices regard screw shots (shots with backspin) as akin to magic, when in reality they are quite simple. Photograph 15 (p. 30) shows where the tip should strike the cue-ball for a screw shot. Note that the cue is as nearly as possible horizontal to the bed of the table and remember that it is the top part of the tip which is actually going to come into contact with the rounded surface of the cue-ball. Place a ball on the centre spot and place the cue-ball approximately 9″ from it, between it and a middle pocket. Strike the cue-ball below centre (see diagram 20) at medium pace. Do not jab or strike too low. Follow through so that you 'feel' the cue-ball on the tip of your cue. If you do all these things, the cue-ball will spin back towards or even into the middle pocket, depending on the speed and spin used.

26

13. When applying screw (backspin), lower your bridge slightly to maintain the horizontal angle at which the tip strikes the cue-ball. Hit cleanly through the ball.

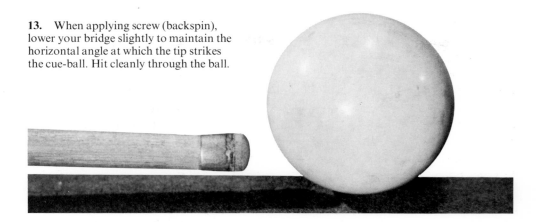

When the cue-ball is struck below centre, it skids backwards towards the object-ball, rather than going over and over like a wheel. On impact with the object-ball, this reverse spin comes into effect and the cue-ball recoils.

The most common mistake with screw shots is to put too much effort into them, getting your arm tense and slamming at the ball, instead of cueing smoothly as you would with an ordinary plain-ball shot. With practise you should find that you are able to control almost to the inch how far you bring the cue-ball back.

Screw shots with the object-ball more than 9″ away are more difficult, because the backspin gradually evaporates the further the cue-ball has to travel before contacting the object-ball. Therefore, the further the object ball is from the cue-ball, the more power is needed and the more important it is to strike as low as possible without miscueing.

STUN

Stun can mean two things: (1) with a straight shot it means stopping the cue-ball dead on impact; (2) with a shot at an angle it means widening the angle at which the cue-ball leaves the object-ball.

When the cue-ball and the object-ball are close together (see diagram 21, shot A), the cue-ball needs only to be struck very slightly below centre

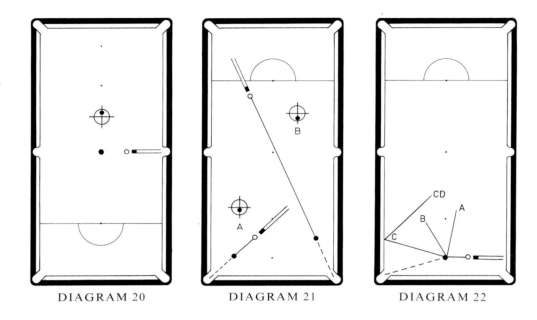

| DIAGRAM 20 | DIAGRAM 21 | DIAGRAM 22 |

to stop it dead. When the balls are further apart, you need to strike much lower (see diagram 21, shot **B**).

In billiards, a great deal of the game can take place round the *red* spot, just as an important part of a frame of snooker can take place round the *black* spot. With this in mind, you should practise potting the red off the spot, not only plain-ball but also with screw, stun and side, thus giving you both certainty of shot in potting and a full range of shot in manoeuvring the cue-ball into the best position to continue your break.

As soon as you get beyond the most elementary level of play, you will realise that positional play is what billiards and snooker are all about. The significance of diagram 22, therefore, is to show the range of positions which are open to a player who has a good command of the basic skills. The range includes anywhere on line **A** (full screw), line **B** (stun), line **C** (plain ball run through) and line **CD** (run through with right-hand side). The area between lines **A** and **B** is also open to lesser degrees of screw.

As you progress, you will develop the touch and control necessary to manoeuvre the cue-ball into the positions you want.

Supplementary Stances, Bridges and Implements

AWKWARD BRIDGES

Billiards and snooker would be easier games if one could always make the perfect bridge. However, because of the cushions and sometimes the position of balls other than the cue-ball, this is impossible. There is, therefore, a series of bridges which you should master for all situations.

Photograph 14 shows a really tricky shot – playing from tight under a cushion. Although the great Joe Davis advocates playing with the fingers flat on the cushion rail, most top players play with the bridge hand slightly raised. The disadvantage of this is that you are striking downwards at the

14. When playing from under the cushion, place as much of the hand as possible on the cushion rail and press downwards on the hand to ensure maximum stability. As only the top part of the cue-ball can be struck with the cue-tip, a slightly downward action is inevitable, but try to keep the cue as horizontal as you reasonably can. As the bridge hand is closer to the cue-ball than it would ordinarily be, it is sometimes advisable to shorten the grip of your right hand on the cue.

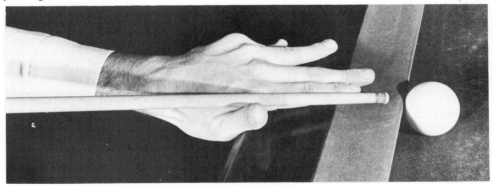

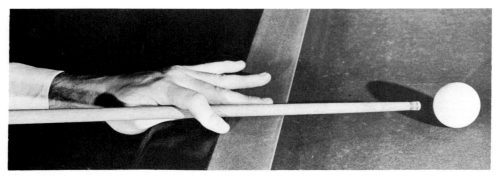

15. When the cue-ball is near the side cushion, the bridge formed by making a loop with the forefinger and tucking the thumb underneath should be used. The cue runs lightly against the thumb and back of the forefinger to prevent it departing from a straight line as it addresses and strikes the ball.

cue-ball, thus exaggerating any unintentional side you may be imparting. You can make this bridge reasonably steady by pressing down on the pads of the fingers, but there is bound to be an element of unsteadiness. Therefore, do not try anything too difficult as regards position when you have to make this bridge and be especially reluctant to employ forcing shots. Concentrate more than usual on keeping still and cut down your backswing, keeping the stroke as brief and simple as possible.

When the cue-ball is a few inches from the cushion there is no particular problem. Make a loop of the first finger so that the cue runs underneath it (see photograph 15). The cue is not quite horizontal to the table and thus the range of screw shots is slightly restricted. For this reason alone, your positional play should usually aim at positioning the cue-ball so that you can make your normal bridge with your hand on the table.

When the cue-ball is slightly further away from the cushion, there is another bridge which can be used. The heel of the hand is pressed firmly against the wood of the cushion rail and the fingers are pressed firmly down on the cushion rail itself. The cue slides against the forefinger (in fact runs parallel to it), with the thumb supporting it the other side.

Bridging over a ball brings out most of the problems that are encountered in playing from under a cushion. Spread your fingers widely and lean downwards on them to give the bridge stability. When the ball intervening between bridge and cue-ball is very close, the bridge will be almost vertical, but

30

16. Front view of the bridge shown in photograph 15. The cue is running through a channel formed by the tip of the second finger and back of the forefinger. Out of sight, the back of the thumb is also helping to keep the cue running on a straight line.

17. A variation of the standard bridge, as the channel for the cue is formed by the thumb and forefinger.

when this space is a few inches neither the bridge nor the cue need to be raised so much. It is even possible in these circumstances to play a simple stun, if the situation demands, but in general it pays to keep the shot as simple as possible.

18

19

20

18. The author shows the advantage of possessing long fingers in this type of position as they make it easier to attain the necessary elevation of the bridge, so that the cue can strike downwards at the available part of the cue-ball. The thumb is turned outwards. The bridge is taken as near as possible to the intervening ball, and the cue, as it strikes downwards, should miss the intervening ball by as small a margin as possible.

19. This front view of Willie Thorne playing over a ball shows the cue just clearing the intervening ball as it strikes the cue-ball. Willie Thorne's fingers are shorter than the author's, so, to gain extra length for his bridge and also to provide extra stability, he rests his forefinger on his second finger. The cue runs both through the channel at the joint of the thumb and across the top of the forefinger.

20. It is helpful if the forefinger is folded onto the second finger to give additional stability and to provide a more secure channel for the cue. The cue has only slight contact with the forefinger. If the cue-ball is even nearer the intervening ball, the bridge has to be balanced on the fingertips, which obviously cannot be quite as steady as the one shown here, where it is possible to get three fingers on the table almost as far as the first finger-joint.

THE REST

The first thing to do when using the rest is to make sure that the equipment is giving you the best possible chance. The best rests have a tight V for the cue to slide in, while the worst have a wobbly U. If there is more than one rest in the room, select the best.

Most novices automatically play with the rest 'tall way up', but this is wrong except possibly for those few shots when you need to strike the cue-ball very high.

Whereas a shot with a normal bridge is made with the right elbow behind the cue, a shot with the rest is made with the elbow swinging sideways to the cue (see photograph 21). With this sideways swing it is more difficult to cue straight but, with practice, it can be managed to the extent that you will be able to play almost as well with the rest as when using a normal bridge.

You should still be sideways to the shot (as with ordinary shots which can be played comfortably without the rest), but the stance is reminiscent of the tennis backhand rather than the forehand. It is not easy to deliver the cue through straight in this position, but most people find it easier if they remember to keep the right elbow up, so that the lower arm is horizontal to the bed of the table.

Photograph 23 shows the cue running on a line which extends right between the eyes. It also shows the cue covering the wooden part of the rest. Some

21 22

21. A different grip and a sideways action is adopted when using the rest. The rest is secured firmly on the table by the left hand, while the right hand grips the cue with the fingers on top and thumb underneath. The heel and palm of the hand face forwards. The cue is slightly elevated, as the screw shot, which is being attempted here, requires a low tip contact on the cue-ball. Since the rest-head is not as flexible as the bridge hand, it cannot be lowered for a screw shot and, therefore, a downward blow has to be struck instead of a horizontal one. As this increases the risk of a miscue, it does not pay to be too ambitious in playing screw shots with the rest, though short-range screws are still fairly easy.

people find this helpful, though it will not be possible if the position of the other balls determines that the rest will have to be placed at an angle to the shot.

Build up your rhythm with several preliminary adresses at the ball and *keep still as you make the actual stroke.*

34

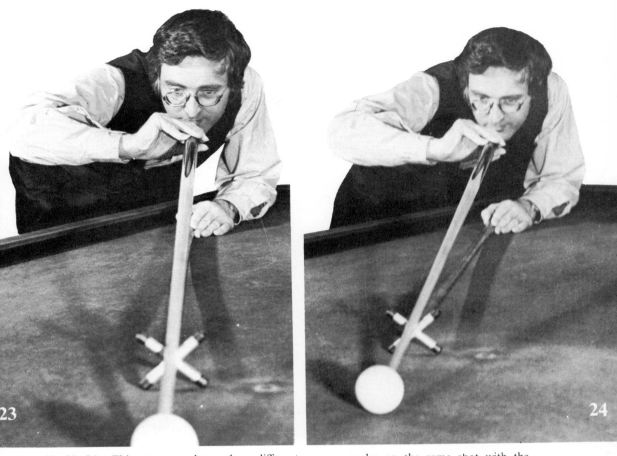

22, 23, 24. This sequence shows three different camera angles on the same shot with the rest (photograph 21). Photograph 23 shows the cue covering the wooden part of the rest. Some players find it useful to check on this (though the position of the ball may sometimes make it impossible), as their preliminary addresses at the cue-ball may reveal that they are cueing slightly at an angle to the shot, rather than hitting straight through it.

SUPPLEMENTARY STANCES

Provided that one foot remains touching the floor until the shot is completed, certain shots which would otherwise require the rest can be made with the orthodox bridge, lifting one leg on to the cushion rail.

When the cue-ball is on the other side of the table you often see players standing stork-like on their left leg with the right leg waving in the air.

35

25, 26. It would be possible for Willie to reach this shot without putting his right leg on the table, but, if he did so, his cue arm would tend to hang away from his body and he would not have the correct alignment of cue, elbow, shoulder and eyes. By climbing on the table, however, Willie shows that it is possible not only to get his shoulder and arm squarely behind the shot but also to rub the cue very lightly against his waistcoat as an aid to keeping the cue on a straight line.

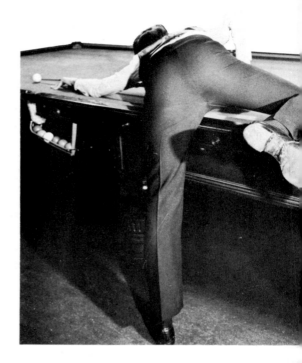

It is almost impossible to stay completely steady on the shot if you stand like this and it is therefore preferable, whenever possible, to put your left leg on the table and let it take your weight, with your right-foot touching the floor (see photographs 27 and 28). This stance enables you to get a horizontal position for the shot, while the stork-like stance merely leaves you looking downwards into the bed of the table, rather than along the line of the shot.

27, 28. Steadiness on the shot is achieved by immobilising every part of the body except the cue-arm.

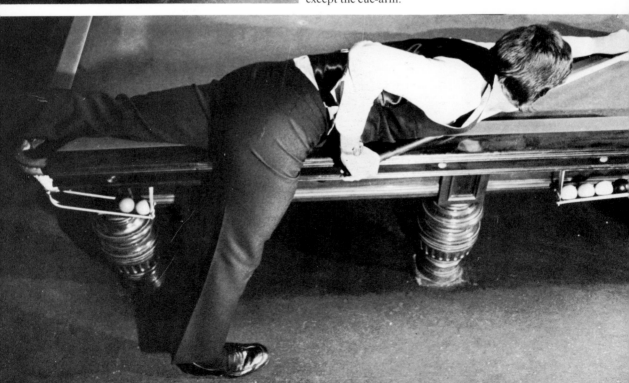

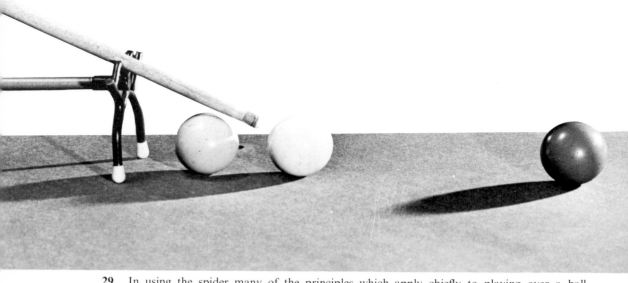

29. In using the spider many of the principles which apply chiefly to playing over a ball with an elevated hand-bridge hold good. The downward slope of the cue should be at just the right angle to miss fouling the intervening ball.

30. This shows a particularly important point in using the spider – the contact must be central, as even the slightest trace of side will be magnified and thus almost impossible to control, because of the downward action of the cue.

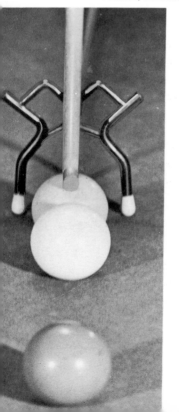

THE SPIDER

The spider is used when the cue-ball is so placed that it cannot be reached using your normal stance and bridge, or when an intervening ball (or balls) prevents you from using the rest.

In photograph 29, the spider could be placed nearer the intervening ball, but this would mean that the cue was striking downwards at a steeper angle, thus making a difficult position more awkward still. As when using the rest, anchor the spider securely to the table with your left hand. Never attempt anything complicated when using the spider, for even the most simple shot with this implement can easily go wrong.

Billiards: An Introduction to Breakbuilding

THE OPENING SHOT

Let us now take the opening of an imaginary game of billiards and see how the various strokes of the game weave into a pattern.

It used to be permissible to begin with a safety miss, but now the player playing the first shot *must* strike the red.

A 'double baulk', i.e. bringing both balls back into baulk so that your opponent cannot play a direct shot at either of them, is possible, but it is usually regarded, even by top players, as so risky (the penalty for failure is usually leaving *both* balls *out* of baulk in a good scoring position) that they generally settle for the shot shown in diagram 23. Played perfectly, the cue-ball will finish tight on the side cushion, with the red near the baulk pocket diagonally opposite, as shown. In this position, it is exceedingly difficult to score or to prevent your opponent from scoring via the easy in-off red next shot, but we will assume that the shot is not quite so good and that there is a reasonable chance of a scoring stroke.

As diagram 24 shows, the shot to play is a cannon, but there is sometimes a problem in that you cannot always play half ball off the white, because the object-white will come off the side cushion and 'kiss' the cue-ball, thus ruining the shot. The solution is to spot further over towards the left-hand side of the D and to play more thinly, as shown in diagram 24.

The cue-ball may complete the cannon in a number of ways and it is as well to recognise that there is an element of chance in where the balls will finish, and whether your next shot will be easy or difficult. We will assume that the balls have run kindly to leave an easy in-off red, a simple half-ball shot, which you will need to play at the right speed to bring the red out of baulk and leave an easy middle pocket in-off (see diagram 25).

39

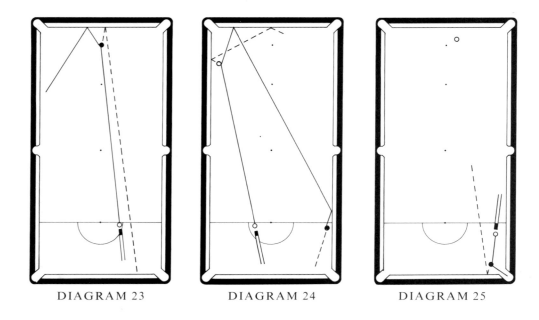

DIAGRAM 23   DIAGRAM 24   DIAGRAM 25

BUILDING A BREAK

The secret of successful billiards is to make one easy shot lead to another easy shot, utilising such basic methods of scoring as the series of middle pocket in-offs to build up your breaks. These 'standard' shots, which, with practise, you will integrate into your game so completely that you will rarely miss them, will not only keep you scoring but will also play you in, giving you the touch and confidence to play the more difficult strokes which may arise later.

Having gone in-off the red and played a few in-offs in the middle pocket, the red may finish too short (diagram 26) for another in-off, but be well placed for either a long in-off or a cannon. Since you must play a cannon at least once every sixteen shots and since in any case it is a mistake to rely too heavily on one scoring method (i.e. in-offs), the shot to play here is a cannon. However, it is not just a question of getting the cannon and taking a chance as to what position is left. Diagram 27 shows what happens

40

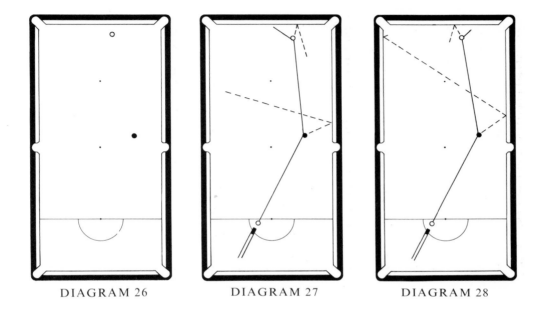

| DIAGRAM 26 | DIAGRAM 27 | DIAGRAM 28 |

if the cannon is played thin (i.e. contacting the red less than half-ball). The red is sliced, as shown, on to the side cushion and finishes in the middle of the table, while the object-white goes down the table, leaving the cue-ball somewhere between them.

Sometimes luck can be on your side and you may have a scoring shot left, but even if you do, your general position will not be as good as if you had played the drop cannon correctly. The drop cannon, as its name implies, drops all three balls relatively close together at the top of the table. This can be done in several ways. In this particular position a contact slightly thicker than half-ball is necessary on the red to double it towards the opposite corner pocket (see diagram 28).

This shot requires good judgment of angles, not only to make the cannon but also to make it in the correct way. The shot must also be played at a well-judged strength. It is no good, for instance, playing at speed, merely to be sure of the cannon, and sending the balls flying everywhere. Diagram 28, however, shows one of the positions in which the balls may finish with a well-placed shot.

41

Another common position is shown in diagram 29, where, following the golden rule of keeping the game as simple as possible, the shot to play is the in-off, sending the object-white up the table off the side cushion for another drop cannon (shot 1). The only pitfalls to avoid here are playing the shot too softly (in which case the red will finish under the cushion and prevent you playing an easy natural drop cannon) or playing it too hard (which will again spoil your intended next shot, the drop cannon, though you will have the chance of a long in-off).

Because the half-ball in-off is such a fundamental stroke in billiards, players tend to find the half-ball angle an easy one to strike in cannon play too. The half-ball angle also makes for ease of positional control, since a perfectly struck half-ball will mean that the speed of the cue-ball and object-ball after impact are identical. However, a player soon learns to use slightly thinner or, more often, slightly thicker than half-ball angles for drop cannons, often in conjunction with side.

In billiards certain basic shots recur. The certainty of control in these basic shots is one of the cornerstones of success, though one of the fascinations of the game is the innumerable different ways in which they may turn out.

TOP OF THE TABLE

Diagram 29, shot 2, shows that the object-white has finished very close to the spot, with the red easily pottable in the top pocket. This is the kind of position most top players strive for, since it enables them to build big breaks quickly and easily. This method, known as 'top of the table', can be utilised at any time when the red is on its spot and the object-white is behind the spot, i.e. in the 'box' marked by the dotted lines in diagram 30.

Even players of good league standard subscribe to the myth that top of the table is too difficult for them; no sooner do they find themselves in a top-of-the-table position than they look for an in-off, in order to revert to scoring by in-offs and all-round play. Kingsley Kennerley, a fine player who coached the current World Professional Billiards Champion, Rex Williams, in his earlier days, is a great believer in getting players into the

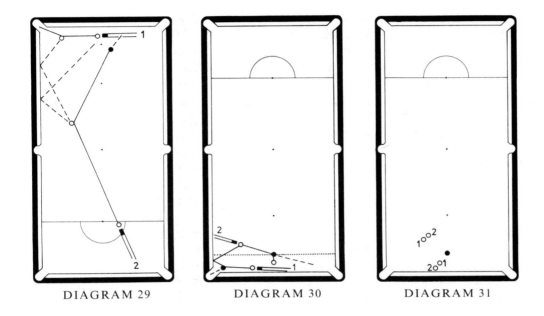

DIAGRAM 29   DIAGRAM 30   DIAGRAM 31

habit of playing top of the table at an early stage of their development. When I went to him for some lessons at the age of fifteen, I believed what I had been told, namely that I should be able to make a 100 break by all-round methods before I should even attempt top of the table. Kennerley quickly demonstrated that this is nonsense and that it is just as valuable for moderate players to make 30 or 40 points at the top of the table as it is for championship-class players to make 200 or 300. There is all the more reason now for moderate players to attempt top of the table than there was ten years ago. Then, if the red was potted twice in succession off its spot, it was placed on the middle spot until it was potted again. This limitation often made it quite difficult to pot the red and get in the right position to play the cannon. However, the red may nowadays be potted *three* times in succession from the spot before it is placed on the middle spot, so one can use the extra available pot not only to build up one's break but also to manoeuvre the cue-ball into position to make the cannon.

Diagram 30, shot 1, shows how the red is potted with the cue-ball crossing the dotted line to leave a cannon from red to white. Shot 2 shows the

43

cue-ball contacting the red almost full on to send it towards the pocket and then cannoning so softly on the object-white that it hardly moves at all. (If the cue-ball remains on the dotted line or inside it, the cannon cannot be made without pushing the red away from a pottable position and knocking the object-white away from the spot.)

The red can now be potted with a simple stun to bring the cue-ball back across the dotted line. (Again, if the cue-ball remains the other side of the dotted line, it is impossible to play a cannon sending the red towards the top pocket. The position left presents the opportunity to pot the red with a stun and to leave the cannon, i.e. virtually the same position as two shots previously.)

As you continue playing these pot-cannon sequences, the object-white goes further from the spot towards the cushion, often at an angle. As it does so (see diagram 31), you will need to remember that the cue-ball will have to be left at an increasingly sharp angle to the red in order to make your cannon. The one thing to avoid at all costs is getting a 5-shot, i.e. the pot and cannon in the same shot, thus ruining your position and forcing you to break away from the top-of-the-table sequence. Sometimes it may be necessary or advisable to bring the red off the side or top cushion so as to leave the pot red (see diagrams 32 and 33).

Diagram 33 shows that it is also possible to make use of the top and side cushions of the pocket, playing the red on to the top cushion approximately 5″ or 6″ from the pocket, so that it strikes the side cushion jaw and comes back into position for a pot. This is admittedly a fairly advanced form of top-of-the-table play (a shot which Norman Dagley, the eleven times English Amateur Billiards Champion, is very good at), but it is possible to make useful breaks at the top without it, particularly if at the first sign of danger you play an in-off in such a way as to enable you to regain top-of-the-table position (see diagram 34). It is easy to pot the red, but impossible to get the cue-ball round for the cannon, because the corner jaw is in the way. Therefore, play to leave the cue-ball on the top jaw of the corner pocket and to leave the half-ball in-off red from the spot. This will take the red up the table for either an in-off or a pot.

If at this point the red is positioned for a pot (diagram 35, p. 46), pot it and take the cue-ball up the table, as shown, into a top-of-the-table position. If the red falls short, play the in-off with the intention of bringing the

44

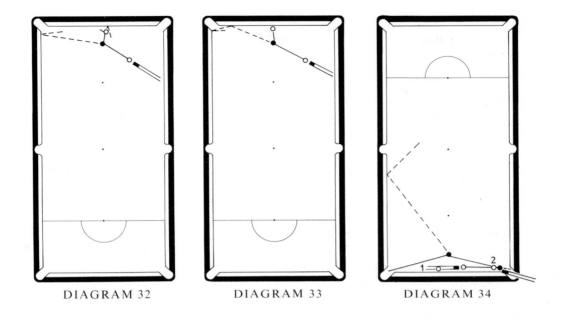

DIAGRAM 32   DIAGRAM 33   DIAGRAM 34

red back slightly further in order to pot it. It is also possible to regain top-of-the-table position by means of a drop cannon, but, since this means that the second object-ball must also be disturbed, this method is rather more chancy in terms of position than potting the red to *leave* the cannon. It is, in fact, the difference between having to control three balls rather than two.

When you have made a few points at the top of the table, the object-white may finish in the type of position shown in diagram 36. This is, incidentally, an excellent position in which to place the balls for practice. If you can make 40 or 50 points regularly, it will mean that you are developing the quality of touch necessary for a successful top-of-the-table player.

POSTMAN'S KNOCK

The first shot, as diagram 36 shows, is a cannon from red to object-white, bringing the red off the side cushion. In making full contact on the object-

45

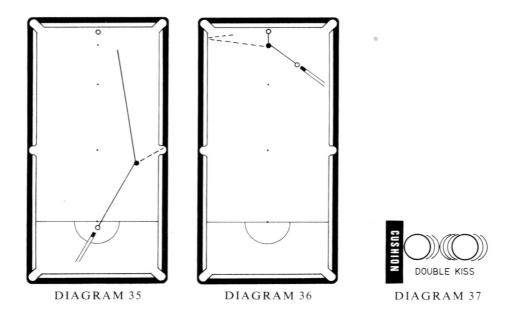

DIAGRAM 35   DIAGRAM 36   DIAGRAM 37

white, the cue-ball will ricochet back. You will hear two clicks in quick succession: the usual one first as the cue-ball contacts the object-white and then the second (the object-white having rebounded from the cushion) as the balls meet again. This shot and this position are known as the 'postman's knock' (see diagram 37).

Having made the cannon, make sure, in potting the red, that you get across the imaginary dotted line, because you must already be thinking of your next cannon. As long as you finish almost anywhere across the dotted line, you should have the opportunity of another pot red; some players indeed make a practice of taking two pots before getting into position for the cannon. Diagram 38 shows how you have failed to leave the cannon, but can do so as you take the 3 points for potting the red with a stun shot.

In general, though, too much potting tends to upset the fluency which is one of the secrets of good play at the top of the table.

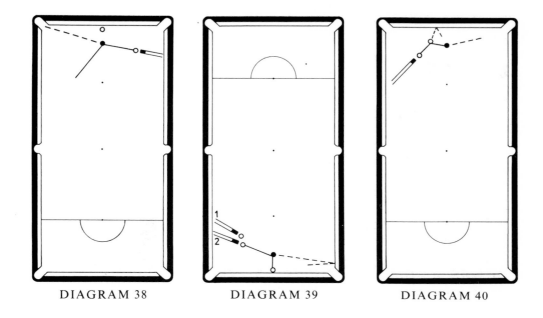

DIAGRAM 38   DIAGRAM 39   DIAGRAM 40

Diagram 39 shows that the cue-ball has not come quite far enough (i.e. to position 1) to play a repeat of the plain cannon full on the object-white, but the same shot can be achieved from position 2 by using strong right-hand side to throw the cue-ball wider. Manoeuvring the cue-ball into the right position for the cannon not only develops your judgment of strength but will also be invaluable in snooker when operating round the black spot, which is vital in compiling big breaks.

The Indian Champion, Michael Ferreira, is a particularly fine exponent of the postman's knock which, although skilful, exploits a relatively limited range of shots.

FLOATING WHITE

The 'floating white' technique is more complex, more varied and, I find, more satisfying to play, though it contains many traps. Diagrams 40–43 illustrate some of the basic 'floating white' moves.

47

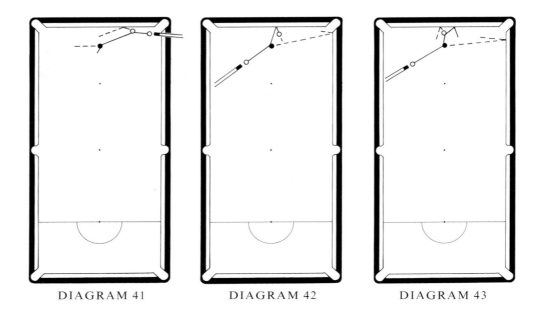

DIAGRAM 41   DIAGRAM 42   DIAGRAM 43

Diagram 40 shows that the object-white has strayed a few inches from the spot. You should, therefore, pot the red to leave a half-ball cannon, as shown, to nudge the object-white on and off the top cushion, back behind the spot – the ideal top-of-the-table position discussed earlier with diagram 29, shot 2.

Diagram 41 shows another way of restoring the object-white to the ideal position. This shot is a little more delicate, because the half to three-quarter ball contact on the red, as the cue-ball goes across it, requires more judgment and touch. If the contact on the red is too thick or too thin, it can spell disaster and the use of side can increase the possibility of a mistake. It is thus worth taking the trouble to position the cue-ball as precisely as you can when potting the red in order to leave the plain ball cannon.

Diagram 42 shows the basic cannon off the top cushion, which is another way of keeping the object-white near the spot. Again, the groundwork is laid by the way the red is potted with a stun to leave a natural angle to ball-cushion-ball. A common fault is to make too thin a contact on the red, which tends to leave an awkward thin cut-back pot red for your

48

next shot. Make sure that you push the red towards the side cushion, 5″ or 6″ from the pocket, and complete the cannon gently by moving the object-white a couple of inches towards the spot. Whenever possible, play with a touch of right-hand side, so that the cue-ball can get right behind the red to make a cannon, which will nudge the object-white nearer the spot, rather than send it diagonally away from it.

Diagram 43 shows a position which could lead to postman's knock by making a full-ball contact on the object-white to leave it dead on the top cushion. Instead, you can play half ball to knock the object-white on and off the top cushion and leave it behind the spot.

There are an infinite number of variations of top of the table, which is a facet of the game which has the merit of being fun to practise by yourself. Even if you fail to conquer all its mysteries, it is a phase of the game which it is much better to know and play a little than not at all.

Billiards: Other Aids to Breakbuilding

Once you can play middle pocket and top pocket in-offs, can pot reasonably well from the spot and are conversant with screw, stun and side, you will gradually be able to add a number of useful shots to your game.

MORE BASIC IN-OFFS

First, let us deal with some in-offs, the backbone of billiards, because, as we have seen, an in-off usually gives a player a wide margin of error in gaining position for his next shot. After an in-off, because the cue-ball may be spotted anywhere in the D, either or both object-balls need only be in the centre of the table (see diagram 44) for you to follow with an easy pot or in-off.

It is for this reason that top players, when they are struggling to keep a break going and when the red is on its spot, very often play to leave the cue-ball on or close to the four lines shown in diagram 45. These lines to the red all provide a basic half-ball in-off red, which is bound to leave the red well placed to continue the break, unless it is hit much too hard and put in baulk. Even when the cue-ball is not positioned precisely on these lines, the in-off is still feasible within limits, if you use extra power, side or, occasionally, both.

If the cue-ball finishes on line A, the in-off can still be played half-ball, if you use check (left-hand) side. The spin will not only narrow the angle at which the cue-ball leaves the red but will also pull it towards the top cushion. Finally, the left-hand side will spin it off the far (i.e. side cushion) jaw of the pocket, into the pocket itself.

When the cue-ball finishes on line B, right-hand (running) side is needed to widen the angle at which the cue-ball leaves the object-ball, though the

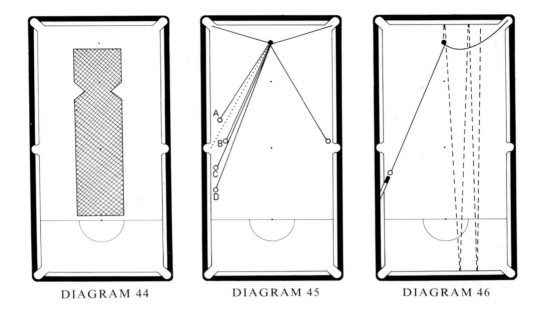

DIAGRAM 44   DIAGRAM 45   DIAGRAM 46

same widening of the angle can be achieved by playing the in-off more briskly and bringing the red in and out of baulk. The snag about the latter method (and indeed many forcing strokes) is that the red has a tendency to finish in baulk, as it is very difficult to control the speed of the red (and thus its final position) when any great power is used.

However, when the cue-ball finishes on line C, the angle is too wide for the in-off to be possible merely with the use of side, so a forcing stroke has to be used. The reason why this is known as a 'swing' in-off will be obvious from diagram 46. Whenever the cue-ball and the object-ball meet at any angle except full ball or almost full ball, a 'throw' or 'bounce' occurs. In other words, instead of the cue-ball coming away from the object-ball on a straight line (as most table diagrams show for the sake of convenience), it describes a curve. The more powerful the stroke, the more pronounced the curve. As soon as the cue-ball loses its initial speed, the curve disappears and the ball travels on a straight line. Thus, with forcing strokes which widen the angle, the shot has to be completed (in this case by the cue-ball entering the pocket) before the curve or swing has gone.

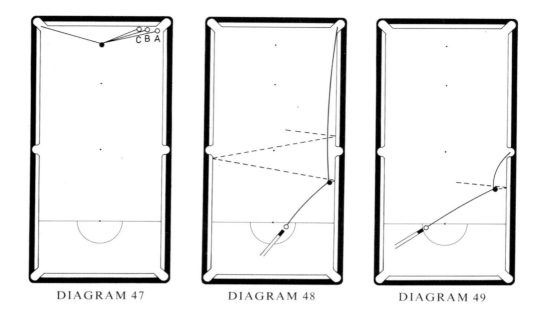

DIAGRAM 47   DIAGRAM 48   DIAGRAM 49

The wider the angle, the more power is required – bearing in mind also that, unless a solid half-ball contact is made, there will be insufficient curve or swing created to complete the shot successfully. With very wide swing in-offs (see diagram 45 line D) running (right-hand) side is also necessary to widen the throw from the red. However, it must be emphasised again that forcing swing in-offs not only can be missed more frequently than those played at medium speed but also leave the ultimate position of the red largely to chance. Good players always play to leave the cue-ball on or very near line A and they generally regard having to play very wide or very narrow in-offs as a sign that their positional play has gone wrong.

The other basic in-off is from the two corner pockets (see diagram 47). As the lines A, B and C show, this shot can be played without any side or with extreme side, depending on the precise position of the cue-ball. Another factor in this shot is the condition of the cloth. Side reacts more strongly on fairly new cloth with a thick nap than it does on older cloth which has had more wear, and the amount of side used must be adjusted accordingly.

52

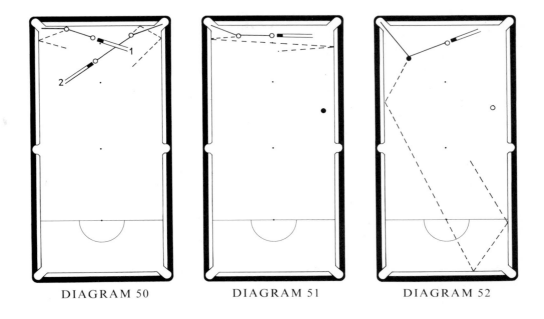

DIAGRAM 50   DIAGRAM 51   DIAGRAM 52

JENNIES AND OTHER IN-OFFS WITH SIDE

More difficult than the so-called 'cross in-offs' just discussed are the long jenny and the short jenny. The secret of both these shots lies in using plenty of check side.

The long jenny should be played briskly and, provided it is carrying enough side, the cue-ball will strike 3″ or 4″ along the side cushion and still spin into the pocket off the top jaw (see diagram 48).

The short jenny calls for more precision and much less speed than the long jenny. As the cue-ball loses it momentum after striking the object-ball, the side should help it curl into the pocket, missing the near jaw, and, still carrying plenty of spin, drop into the pocket off the far jaw (see diagram 49).

The run-through with side is another in-off which is invaluable in keeping a break going. When the object-ball is on a cushion (as shown in diagram 50, shot 1), the in-off, with practice, is quite simple. You should strike above centre with right-hand side (as always when using side, pushing the

53

cue through the right-hand side of the ball and not brushing across it), contacting the red about three-quarter ball. The cue-ball will then run through, hugging the cushion, because of the side it is carrying, and drop into the pocket.

The variation shown in diagram 50, shot 2, is slightly more difficult, because the object-ball is further away from the cushion. However, the principle of the shot, i.e. extreme check (in this case, left-hand) side, is the same even though the cue-ball, because of the different angle, will have to touch the cushion much nearer the pocket in order to enter it than in shot 1.

Another extremely useful, but more difficult, run-through in-off is the one with running side shown in diagram 51. Here, right-hand side has to be used, making a nearly full contact on the object-white, with the intention of spinning the cue-ball into the pocket off the side cushion jaw.

There are many occasions when combinations of screw and side need to be used in in-offs. Diagram 52, for instance, is a shot which recurs frequently. It is possible to play this shot half-ball with no side, but this will leave the red in baulk. It is much better to play thinner, with running (right-hand) side, to give the object-ball (the red) a wider angle off the cushion and thus bring it out of baulk. However, the nearer the object-ball gets to the side cushion, the more difficult it is to play in-offs with running side, because, if the cue-ball catches the top cushion jaw of the pocket, the right-hand side will keep it out of the pocket rather than help it in. In diagram 53, for example, the in-off is impossible with right-hand side but, with practice, it is quite easy with screw and left-hand side. Play quarter-ball with screw and left-hand side, and the cue-ball will hug the cushion, because of the side it is carrying, and spin into the pocket.

OTHER USES OF SIDE

The uses of side, screw and stun in cannon play and potting are less easy to categorize.

As diagram 54 shows, running (left-hand) side can be used to widen the angle the cue-ball takes from the object-ball in order to complete a cannon,

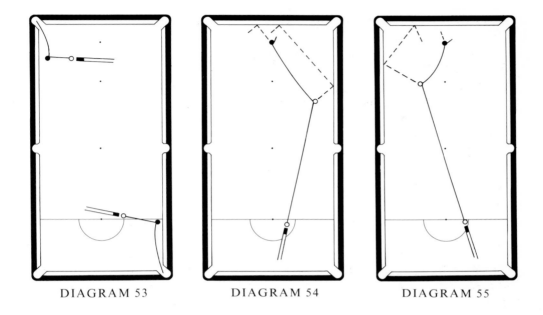

DIAGRAM 53   DIAGRAM 54   DIAGRAM 55

since, in this position, the plain ball attempt at the cannon would result in the cue-ball going inside the red.

Diagram 55 shows the use of check (left-hand) side to complete another drop cannon.

Side is, however, more often used by players as a means of improving position. In diagram 56, for instance, you can place the cue-ball as indicated and play the straightforward ball-to-ball plain cannon. As the dotted lines show, this will leave the cue-ball between the two object-balls and awkwardly placed to continue your break. If you spot the cue-ball as in diagram 57, the difference is immediately apparent. Because the angle is wider, you will need strong right-hand side to complete the cannon, but the object-white will also be thrown wider and will bounce off the side cushion in such a way as to leave both object-balls nicely in front of the cue-ball.

The early part of this chapter was devoted to the ways in which players look for a basic half-ball in-off when they are in doubt as to the best way of keeping the break going.

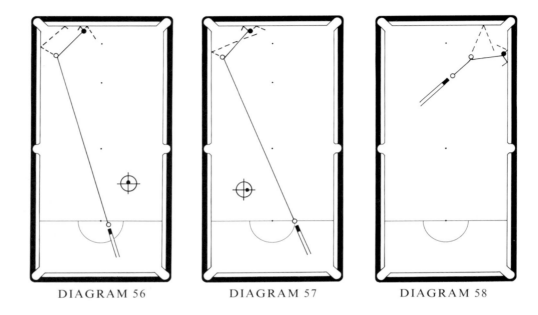

DIAGRAM 56   DIAGRAM 57   DIAGRAM 58

THE GATHERING SHOT

Another basic ploy is the 'gathering' shot, so called for reasons which are obvious in diagram 58. This particular shot is played strongly enough to bring the object-white back from the top cushion towards the red, as shown. The precise position in which the ball will finish after a more difficult gathering shot – as when one of the object-balls has to be sent round the table off two or three cushions – may be more awkward to predict, but, if you can develop enough touch to get all three balls to finish in a fairly small area, you will be most unlucky if you are not left a reasonably easy way of continuing your break.

56

Snooker : Breakbuilding

RED – BLACK BREAKBUILDING

A player who has a good grounding in billiards starts with a great advantage over a snooker player who has never played billiards at all. This advantage is seen most clearly in his knowledge of the various angles that the cue-ball may take after contacting another ball and in his knowledge of the various cushion angles. Neither of these is of the slightest use in pure potting but, beyond a certain very basic standard, potting means a great deal less than manoeuvring the cue-ball either in safety play or in positioning it in order to continue a break.

As was said earlier, the red in billiards can be potted from its spot in many ways and the cue-ball can be positioned differently by using screw, stun and side. Top players *do* succeed in making brilliant individual pots, but in every case they rely primarily on compiling a break with a series of easy shots once they are 'in'. Whenever a good player is left in a position like the one in diagram 59, in which the black is on its spot and there are three pottable reds near it, he thinks: 'Here's 24, unless I do something silly'. Good players rarely play any shot without a clear idea of what their next shot is going to be. The less experienced the player, the less precisely he will be able to control the cue-ball, though even so he should observe general, if obvious, principles such as keeping the cue-ball off the cushion and avoiding having to bridge over a ball.

Round the black spot, two other factors are particularly important: (a) avoid leaving the cue-ball straight on the black and, (b) clear the paths between the black spot and the top two pockets.

If you examine the shots needed to complete the three reds/three blacks sequence in diagram 59, you will see that the break depends only on two

basic ploys:
(1) leaving an angle
on the black and,
(2) stunning out to
leave the cue-ball
nicely positioned for
the next red. The
diagram shows the
sequence being com-
pleted without the
cue-ball touching a
cushion, but there is
such a large margin
of error that you can
use the cushions to
help you keep
position, if necessary.
There is nothing
intrinsically wrong

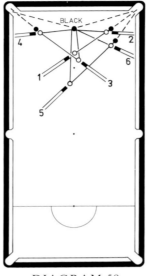

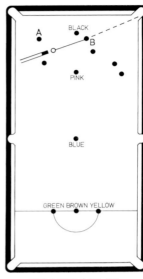

DIAGRAM 59   DIAGRAM 60

in using cushions for position, but it is important to master the technique
of leaving an angle on the black and stunning up the table, because you
will need this skill in controlling the cue-ball in a confined area. The balls
will not always be nicely spaced out (as here). More often there will be
pottable reds mingled with unpottable reds and awkward reds.

Diagram 60 demonstrates an important element in building a break –
choice of shot – which depends less on technical factors than on experience
and common sense. On the face of it, there is a choice between red A
and red B, either of which is easy to pot in such a way as to leave a
perfect position on the black. However, looking further ahead, it becomes
obvious that red B is the better bet, because it leaves the black more open
for later stages in the break.

Diagram 61 also presents a choice between reds. Red B is in the same
position as in diagram 60 and is a high priority in order to give room
for manoeuvre round the black. However, because B is not pottable yet,
you will have to wait your chance for this ball and, meanwhile, from the
available choice of reds, take red A with a little screw and right-hand side

58

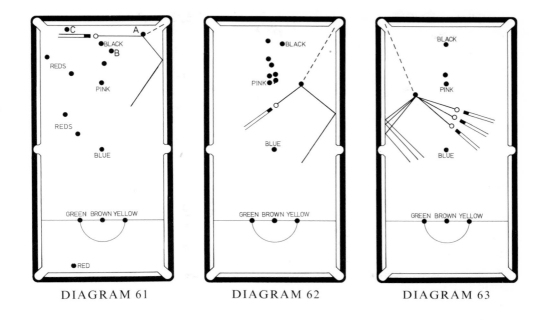

DIAGRAM 61   DIAGRAM 62   DIAGRAM 63

to leave position on the pink. By taking red C it would have been possible to run the cue-ball off the top and side cushions and leave the pink in the middle, but you would still have the problem of red A blocking the black's path to one top pocket later in the break. In short, it stands to reason that it is much easier to build a break round the black spot if the black is pottable into both pockets.

BREAKBUILDING WITH OTHER COLOURS

Although the black plays an important part in most big breaks, there are many occasions when the black is tied up among a cluster of other balls or is awkwardly placed on a cushion. There are in addition countless occasions when the position of the other balls makes it impossible, or not worthwhile, to attempt to get position on the black.

The blue is often an invaluable ball with which to link a break together. As diagram 62 shows, the black and pink are hemmed in, thus, in potting

59

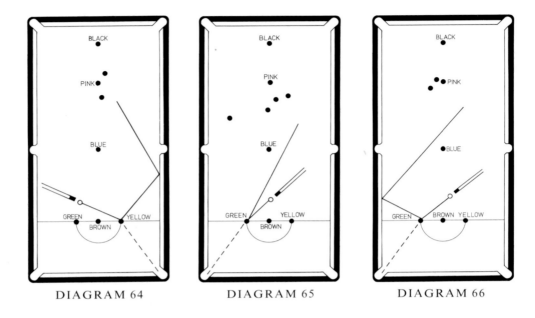

DIAGRAM 64   DIAGRAM 65   DIAGRAM 66

the red, the idea is to get position slightly baulk-side of the blue, so that you can easily take the cue-ball up for another loose red. Play with screw and a little right-hand side to widen the angle that the cue-ball takes when it hits the side cushion. If you play without this touch of side, you will have to screw nearer the middle pocket (which can be a dangerous thing to do if you slightly over-screw) or bring the cue-ball further away from the side cushion, in towards the blue (which can leave you too close to the blue and force you to pot it at an acute angle).

There are countless variations on this type of shot, which are well worth some systematic practice. Practise potting reds (see diagram 63) into the corner pocket from all angles between quarter to three-quarter ball to leave an identical position on the blue. The thinner screws require very good touch, as you will need to make the screw and side 'bite' sharply, even though you will be hitting the cue-ball quite softly.

It is also useful to practise screwing up the table for the reds from the baulk colours: the yellow, green and brown (see diagram 64). Because the cue-ball is travelling several feet, its final position is more difficult to gauge

60

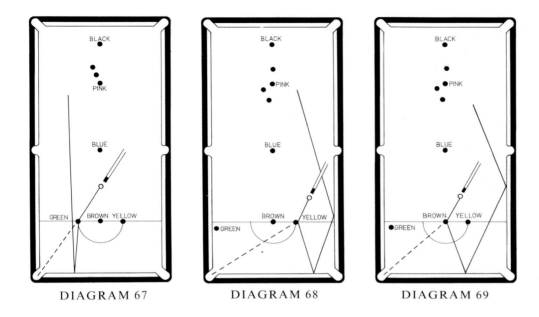

DIAGRAM 67   DIAGRAM 68   DIAGRAM 69

than for a shorter distance, but again with practice a fair degree of control can be obtained. Screwing off the green and yellow is frequently preferable to screwing off the brown, as the middle pocket all too often seems to get in the way.

Diagram 65 shows a straightforward screw back from a three-quarter ball contact on the green. In diagram 66, however, the different angle on the green (i.e. half-ball instead of three-quarter ball) means that you will have to use the side cushion. Play this shot with screw and some right-hand side, but be careful not to overdo the latter, as the remaining red will not be pottable if the cue-ball runs much further than the position shown in the diagram. Diagram 67 is another three-quarter ball pot on the green, but this time the position of the two remaining reds, between the pink and black spots, makes it necessary to play the run-through instead of the screw back. Make sure you strike the cue-ball well above centre. Unintentional stun or inadvertent use of a little left-hand side (check) will restrict the run of the cue-ball and leave it short of the desired position on the reds.

61

Diagram 68 shows the brown being potted with a touch of left-hand side to swing the cue-ball off the baulk and side cushions in towards the two remaining reds. Without the side, the cue-ball would finish much nearer the side cushion and make your next shot more difficult. Most good players in fact prefer, if there is a choice, to play positional shots which bring the cue-ball away from a cushion towards the next object-ball rather than shots in which the cue-ball is travelling towards a cushion.

Diagram 69 is similar to diagram 68 – your choice of the yellow is determined by the fact that a straight screw back from the brown will land the cue-ball in the middle pocket.

Snooker: Choosing Your Shot

CHOICE OF SHOT

What was said in the previous chapter on red-black breakbuilding is also broadly true of the pink and other balls. Once you start thinking: 'Yes, if I take this red now, that other red will be pottable later in the break', there is some justification for feeling that you have the beginnings of a snooker brain.

In diagram 70 the choice of red is determined not by the need to create space round the black spot but by the chance of allowing a greater margin for error in positional play. Red A is the ball to take here (not red C), because in so doing it becomes possible to pot red B in both top pockets instead of only in one.

In any class of play, confidence in easy and not very difficult shots, both in potting and positional play, is more important long term than flashes of brilliance. More important still, it is generally the case that, if a player gradually builds up his confidence with easy shots, he is more likely to pot something difficult than if he has been missing shots he ought to get.

There are times when one is forced into playing 'neck or nothing' shots but, generally speaking, it is wise to balance the risk of leaving an easy opening for your opponent against the possible gain if you are successful with your initial shot. For instance, in diagram 71 some inexperienced players might attempt red A, rolling the cue-ball the length of the table, in order to pot the red slowly and stay on the black. Even if you sight the angle correctly and stroke the cue-ball perfectly (two big ifs), the slightest imperfection in the table will cause the cue-ball to run off course before it reaches the red and thus ruin the shot. If this happens, your opponent has the choice of two easy shots and the chance of a useful break.

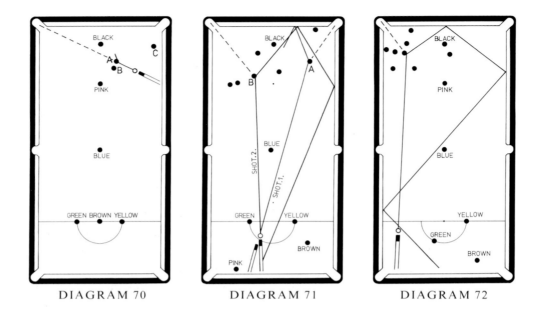

DIAGRAM 70   DIAGRAM 71   DIAGRAM 72

SHOTS TO NOTHING

In the sort of position described above, it is much more sensible to attempt red B (diagram 71). If you pot it, the brown or (as the cue-ball has run slightly further) the pink is available to continue your break; if you do not succeed then at least the cue-ball will be near the baulk cushion, keeping your opponent at a distance from the reds.

These 'shots to nothing', so called because they offer the maximum gain for the minimum risk, are often open to you very early in a frame, if you look for them. In diagram 72, for example, it may not be immediately obvious that a red can be potted into the top pocket despite the cluster of reds round it. These 'shots to nothing' call for good judgment of angles, since they will be completely spoiled if the cue-ball kisses other balls en route to the baulk cushion. Billiards players start with an advantage here, since they are so accustomed to attempting cannons that they are naturally more adept at avoiding them when they want to. In this particular case, you should attempt the pot with some right-hand side, both to help swing

64

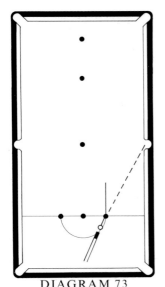

DIAGRAM 73

the cue-ball round the black and also to avoid kissing the blue on the way back down the table.

TAKING THE COLOURS

Whatever has happened in the early stages of a frame can often be reversed at the colours' stage, when all the reds have been potted. In other words, you can either throw away a winning position or retrieve a lost one. The six colours total 27 points, a higher reward for potting six balls than even three reds and three blacks. At local championship standard or higher it is not unusual to have all the colours on their spots at the end of a frame, so it is useful to spend some time practising clearing the table from this position. Even when only some of the colours are on their spots, this practice will pay dividends. The first shot, the yellow, is not difficult, but it demands care even from good players.

Except when they have the full face of the pocket to aim at, most players find it more difficult to pot into the middle pockets than into the corner pockets. The corner pockets are placed at the convergence of two lines, whereas the middle pockets are on a straight line. Middle pockets are shaped differently from corner pockets, so that with a pot such as the yellow from its spot it is as well to aim slightly at the far jaw rather than for the full face of the pocket. If the yellow just catches the near jaw, it has little chance of entering the pocket, but, by playing on to the inside of the far jaw, the cut of the pocket should help the ball in.

You will note that in diagram 73 the cue-ball has been placed in the D at a slight angle to the yellow, rather than dead straight. This is to keep the cue-ball more in the centre of the table and thus nearer the next ball, the green. The further the cue-ball strays in positional play from the next object-ball, the more difficult the pot becomes. The more difficult the pot becomes, the more concentration you will need merely to pot it, so the chances are that, even if you do pot it, your position for your third shot will be even worse.

65

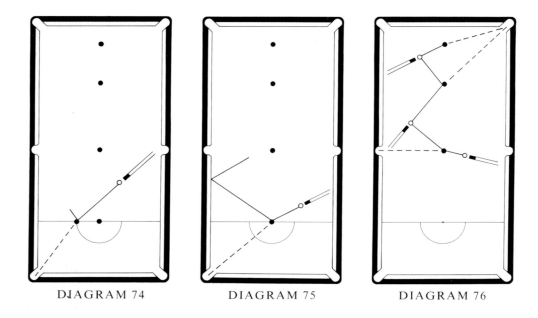

DIAGRAM 74   DIAGRAM 75   DIAGRAM 76

When potting the yellow, make sure that the cue-ball runs through sufficiently to leave it with at least a half-ball angle on the green. Anything thinner than that makes the pot more difficult and the cue-ball more difficult to control.

Players generally pot better when they have both the object-ball and the pocket in vision; this is always the case with straight or three-quarter ball shots. The thinner the pot becomes (under three-quarter ball), the nearer the object-ball has to be to the pocket to have the cue-ball or the object-ball and the pocket in vision simultaneously. It is for this reason that potting into a 'blind' pocket is always a little more difficult than potting into a visible pocket.

Assuming that you have played the yellow correctly, you should be able to stun in the green to leave an angle on the brown (see diagram 74). Stun in the brown to leave an angle on the blue (see diagram 75), then roll the blue in slowly. Stun in the pink and pot the black (see diagram 76). This is a perfect clearance of the colours without once getting into difficulty, but there are other sequences which are no less perfect. For in-

66

stance, in potting the yellow, the cue-ball may have travelled further up the table to leave a straight green. The green, therefore, has to be played using screw with the intention of leaving the stun brown, as in the 'ideal' sequence described before. Practise clearing the colours and you will find yourself gradually incorporating into your repertoire all types of positional shots, which are equally valuable earlier in the game.

One often hears admiring comments like, 'That was a good pot. It didn't touch the sides', but, in fact, except when there is a completely open pocket to aim at, almost every pot does touch at least one jaw of the pocket. Pockets vary from the very difficult to the very easy. This depends more on their shape than on their size. Pockets are required by the rules to be $3\frac{1}{2}''$ across at the fall (or lip) of the pocket, but it is the shape of the inside jaw of the pocket which is all-important. If the inside jaw is cut away so that the pocket opens out towards the back, a ball will 'throw' into the pocket after hitting the jaw. If, however, the opening of the pocket narrows after the fall, the jaws of the pocket tend to throw a ball out. When you play on a strange table, it is worthwhile giving the shape of the pockets a little preliminary study so that you know in advance what sort of liberties you can take with them.

Snooker: Tactics

CORRECTING FAULTS

The limit of a player's development usually depends on the quality of his basic technique – straight cueing, stillness on the shot, accurate striking of the cue-ball and other dull-sounding but vital attributes. If, for example, after a great deal of practice, you still find the positions described in the last chapter beyond you, go back to basics. Are you standing correctly? Is your bridge firm? Is your cueing 'over the spots' accurate?

If you can satisfy yourself on these points and yet you still find you are having trouble, line up a series of straight pots into the top pockets, putting reds on the imaginary line between the blue spot and the middle pockets, and the cue-ball in a straight line about 2′ away (see diagram 77). As your success rate increases, move the cue-ball progressively further away until it is on the baulk line. If you can consistently pot straight reds from this position, there is nothing much wrong with the straightness of your cueing.

To practise angled shots put a ball on the pink spot and the cue-ball just inside either the yellow or green spot (see diagram 78). It is essential to pot from both sides otherwise you may develop a preference for one side or the other as some slight irregularity in your stance or sighting creeps in.

Many players have particular difficulty with shots which are almost, but not quite, straight (see diagram 79). Again, play a series of these. If you are missing consistently, the chances are that you are allowing *too much* angle and are making the object-ball strike several inches up the side cushion.

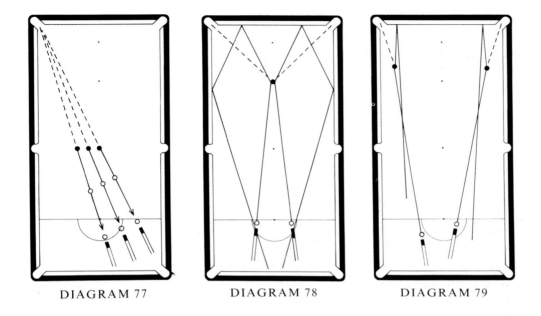

| DIAGRAM 77 | DIAGRAM 78 | DIAGRAM 79 |

These 'almost straight shots' are even straighter than I thought when I first played and it took a lot of self-discipline to adjust my mind to the fact that my initial eyesight assessment of this angle had been incorrect. I concentrated on hitting this sort of shot fuller and fuller until, in the end, I had the correct angle imprinted so deeply in my memory that my assessment of the angle became subconscious.

John Spencer, who has three times won the World Professional Snooker Championship, has rightly said, 'Potting is memory'. In other words, by storing the information in your mind from potting a ball, you recognise a particular potting angle when it recurs, even if the shot is in a different part of the table. However, even the best memory for potting angles is useless if your cue action is inaccurate, so keep practising until it is as grooved and straight as you can make it.

Let us now chart a few recurrent situations, common positions and choices of shot with which players frequently have to deal.

BREAKING OFF

The first shot of a frame is very important. If you win the toss, always break off, because you have a first-class chance of taking the initiative straight away. The most reliable opening shot is to strike the outside red with right-hand side, to bring the cue-ball off three cushions to within an inch or so of the baulk cushion behind the green (see diagram 80). Unless you are very careless (if, for example, you do not use enough right-hand side and the cue-ball collides with the blue) this shot cannot go seriously wrong and may well get your opponent off on the wrong foot by giving him a tricky first shot.

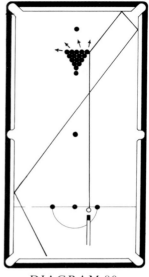

DIAGRAM 80

THE OPENING EXCHANGES

The opening exchanges in most frames consist of both players trying to get the cue-ball to return as near as possible to the baulk cushion, until one player either makes a mistake and leaves an opening or takes a risk and tries to pot a red from a long distance. Occasionally, the reds may split from the opening shot in such a way that your opponent cannot make his return to the baulk cushion. In diagram 80 he does not have this problem, but he is seriously impeded by having the cue-ball right under the baulk cushion. It is difficult enough in any circumstances to play from under the cushion, since you can only hit the top part of the cue-ball, but the difficulty is magnified when the object-ball is some distance away.

The answering shot in this tricky position is the very thin contact shot shown in diagram 81. At first glance there seems to be grave danger of an in-off, but your 'billiards' experience should tell you that the angle for this is almost half-ball. If you hit the shot much thinner, there is no danger of an in-off and the cue-ball, with good judgment of strength, should return near the baulk cushion. This very thin escape occurs a great deal and is,

70

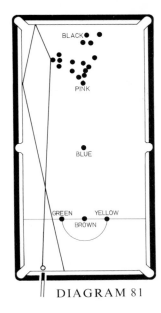

DIAGRAM 81

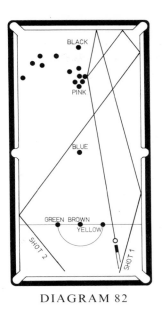

DIAGRAM 82

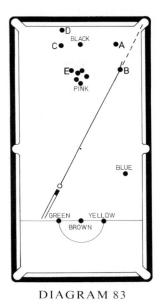

DIAGRAM 83

therefore, one to be mastered. Indeed, most safety shots from the reds at this stage of the game are thinner than half-ball.

Except when you are in extreme difficulty, always try to answer a good safety shot with a better one. There will be times when you must simply concentrate on preventing your opponent from scoring, but otherwise you should always play your safety shots constructively. In diagram 82, for example, many players would play the thin return (shot 1), which is correct as far as it goes, but which gives your opponent a chance to make a similar reply. Shot 2 is much better because, by playing with right-hand side, the cue-ball can be swung round off three cushions to the opposite side of the table, where the distribution of the reds is such that a return to the baulk cushion is impossible.

What can happen when a thicker than half-ball contact is made is shown in diagram 83, where the cue-ball has only returned half-way down the table and the more thickly contacted red has disturbed the pack, leaving the type of middle distance pot which often leads to a break.

MORE CHOICES OF SHOT

There is, in fact, a choice of reds in diagram 83. Superficially, red A may seem preferable – it is nearer the pocket than red B and the cue-ball has only to bounce off the top cushion gently to finish in position for the black. The trouble is, though, that gently played rolls, particularly when the cue-ball has some distance to travel before contacting the object-ball, are exceedingly treacherous not only as we have seen for potting but also in controlling the cue-ball. Red B, however, is our old friend, the straight pot. Stun this in – as you should if you are cueing straight – and you should go into the lead with a useful break.

The angle on the black is such that you could pot it at speed, so that the cue-ball would rebound off the top cushion and scatter the reds, possibly

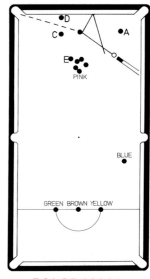

DIAGRAM 84

paving the way for a really big break. However, even top professionals would rarely split the pack so early in a break. They would instead make sure of clearing the 'open' reds and, only when there was one or possibly two of these left, would they consider opening the pack. The theory behind this is that it is better to make as sure as one can of 20 or 30 points, rather than make 8 and perhaps leave oneself in an impossible position. The angle on the black is such that reds C, D or A can easily be taken after it. D is the most difficult of the three, so it is sensible on most occasions to take the easier reds first. A is easy to play for, but C is the best choice (see diagram 84) by means of stunning the cue-ball on and off the top cushion, because potting C will leave the area round the black spot completely clear. This is likely to be important when you come to take red D. Pot C with stun to leave a slight angle on the black, so that another stun will leave you in a position to take red A next (see diagram 85, shot 1). When you pot the black (diagram 85, shot 2), try to leave a position such that in potting A (see diagram 86, shot 1), you will position the cue-ball at a slight angle on the black so that you can take red D along the cushion.

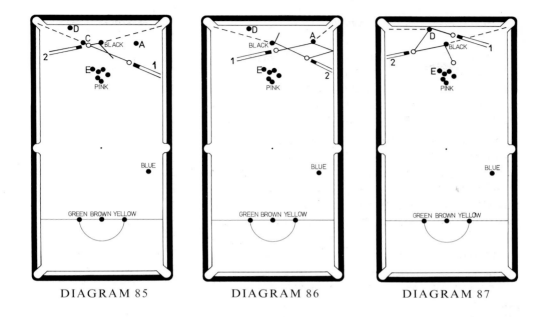

| DIAGRAM 85 | DIAGRAM 86 | DIAGRAM 87 |

This simple little shot shows that the secret of the success of top players is often the precision with which they control the cue-ball in easy shots, rather than their spectacular feats with difficult shots.

In potting the black (see diagram 86, shot 2), play to leave a three-quarter ball red D along the cushion. If you leave yourself straight on this red, it is impossible to obtain good position on the black and cuts along the cushion are notoriously difficult to gauge.

Pot red D firmly to leave position on the black (see diagram 87, shot 1), but do not be too eager to leave an angle to split the pack from the black. First examine carefully whether there is a red which at first glance is part of the pack but which is in reality pottable. Red E is a typical example of this; it is almost part of the pack but is actually pottable in the middle pocket, thus, when potting the black, you should manoeuvre the cue-ball into a three-quarter angle to take red E (see diagram 87, shot 2).

These middle-pocket pots are invaluable in keeping a break going but they do need practice.

73

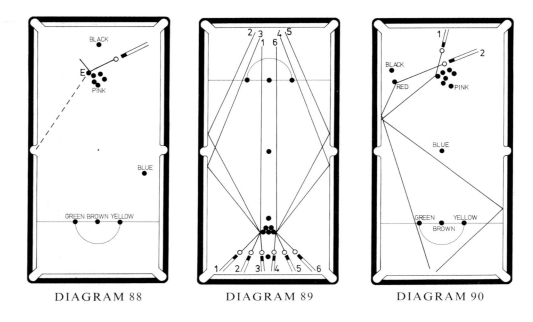

DIAGRAM 88   DIAGRAM 89   DIAGRAM 90

A controlled medium-paced shot with screw (see diagram 88) should leave you on the black with a good chance of splitting the reds. Splitting a large pack of reds is always to some extent a gamble, even if the cue-ball goes into them at a fair speed: the reds may split perfectly for a big break or the cue-ball may end up in the middle of them, with no way of scoring. There is good reason, when this happens, to be thankful that you already have 30 or 40 points on the board!

CONSTRUCTIVE SAFETY

There will be countless occasions when you find yourself near the pack of reds without a really good potting opening, but with an easy chance to leave the cue-ball on the baulk cushion for your opponent. Play these shots with care. Do not just send the cue-ball vaguely down the table, thinking it sufficient to stop your opponent scoring – make things as difficult

74

for him as you can! Get the cue-ball as near as possible to the baulk cushion; if you can get it behind one of the baulk colours, so much the better. There are six shots in diagram 89, all of which should be played with the idea of putting the cue-ball as near the baulk cushion as possible. Shot 1 is a simple quarter- to half-ball flick off the end red, taking the cue-ball between the yellow and brown. In shot 2 the angle is such that a direct route to the baulk cushion is impossible, so the shot must be played from the side cushion to leave the cue-ball on the baulk cushion behind the yellow. Play this with a little screw and right-hand side.

Shot 3, in which the cue-ball is almost directly behind the pack, requires the use of right-hand side to widen the angle at which the cue-ball will leave the side cushion. This is necessary to avoid making contact with the yellow.

Shots 4, 5 and 6 duplicate shots 1, 2 and 3 from the other side of the table. None of them is difficult to execute, but there are clear advantages to be gained by those who play them with good touch, since it is a great deal more difficult to play an answering safety shot if the cue-ball is tight on the baulk cushion than if it is 5″ or 6″ away.

To conclude the hints on this important phase of the game, diagram 90, shot 1 shows the cue-ball being played with left-hand side to bring it off the two side cushions and leave it dead on the baulk cushion. Shot 2 shows left-hand side being used to widen the angle that the cue-ball takes from the cushion to avoid a cannon on the green and to take it again to within 1″ or so of the baulk cushion.

SNOOKERING

Except at the end of a frame when the combined value of the balls remaining is insufficient to win by potting alone, snookering is usually a matter of tactics rather than a device for scoring points. Some players, particularly when they have lost their confidence, pay excessive attention to snookering, forgetting perhaps that in the end they have to pot balls to win.

However, there are also times when discretion is the better part of valour, as in diagram 91. Either through bad luck or bad judgment, you have

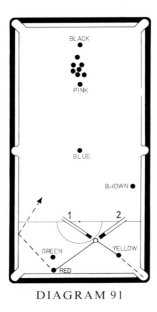

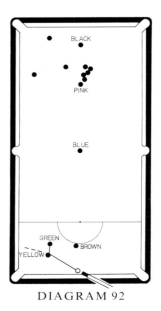

DIAGRAM 91   DIAGRAM 92

potted a red and finished straight on both the green and the yellow, so
that, even with a deep screw, it is impossible to get the cue-ball up the
table and in position for one of the remaining reds. You could either pot
the yellow or the green and then attempt the red along the baulk cushion,
but this is a shot to be very wary of. If played along the *top* cushion,
the nap (which runs from baulk to black end) helps the object-ball hug
the cushion. However, on the baulk cushion, the nap pulls the object-ball
away from the cushion, so the shot is more likely to be missed. Therefore,
your shot is to pot the yellow with a stun stroke and then to stun the
red full to send it up the table, leaving the cue-ball behind the green.

This should prove a very nasty position for your opponent, because the
worst snookers to negotiate are those where the object-balls are in the open
with the obvious danger of conceding an opening for a break. Should your
opponent also be on the cushion, this will intensify his difficulty as he will
be unable to control the use of any side that he needs as accurately as
if he had his bridge hand on the table.

76

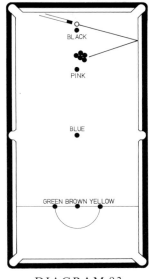

DIAGRAM 93

As explained earlier, 'shots to nothing' on the reds are ideally those shots which will leave a colour on, if the red is potted, but which in any case leave your opponent dead safe or snookered, if it is not. Sometimes, 'shots to nothing' do not quite work out as planned and there may be no colour available to follow the red. Often, however, there is a very good alternative in rolling up slowly behind one of the baulk colours. Judgment of strength is the key to this shot. It is, of course, disastrous not to reach the object-ball, for this will give your opponent the option either of taking a free ball or of asking you to play again. On the other hand, the point of the shot is lost if it is played too hard.

Look carefully at the distribution of the reds before you play a roll up. It can often be, as in diagram 92, that the escape from one side cushion (here, the right) is into a tight pack of reds, while the escape from the other cushion is more dangerous, because some reds are open and pottable. Unless you can leave the cue-ball almost touching the brown, so that *both* escape routes are blocked, it is good policy in this type of position to play the cue-ball from the yellow to leave it behind the green. This will make your opponent use the left-hand side cushion, where the open reds are, or play a more complex two-cushion escape using baulk and side cushions. He will need to be a good player to play the latter accurately enough to deny you an opening.

SNOOKER ESCAPES

The basic rule in escaping from snookers is to roll up slowly to balls which are not pottable and to make firm contact with balls which are in order to have a chance of putting them safe.

In diagram 93 all you have to do is to pick your spot on the side cushion and roll up to the reds. You cannot put your opponent in trouble like

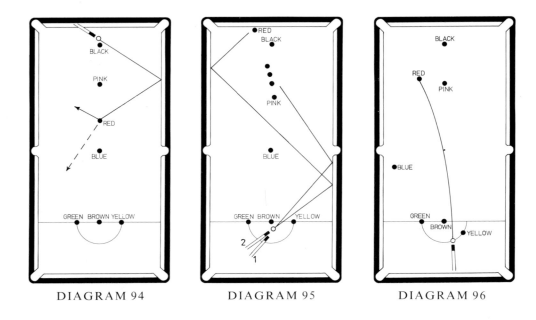

DIAGRAM 94   DIAGRAM 95   DIAGRAM 96

this, but at least he has to play another good shot to put *you* in trouble. Quite the worst thing to do is to scatter the reds and present him with a break. However, when the snookered red at which you are playing is in the open, it is clearly madness to roll up to it slowly, for even if you hit it, you will leave it on for your opponent. It is better to play this escape briskly (see diagram 94). If you miss the red, the cue-ball will at least be travelling further away from it for your opponent. If you hit it, the force of the contact should again put some distance between the two balls.

As shown in diagram 95, you will frequently find it advantageous, when snookered, to attempt to escape on to a difficult isolated red (shot 2) rather than on to a more obvious red or group of reds (shot 1). You must attempt to escape from snookers, but it is often better to risk giving away 4 points and leaving your opponent safe, rather than to negotiate the snooker and leave your opponent a frame-winning break. In diagram 95, for example, it is clearly wise to try to hit the 'safe' red on the cushion rather than the open reds round the pink spot.

78

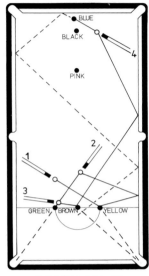

DIAGRAM 97

The swerve shot sometimes provides an alternative method of escape and it is best employed when the escape is on to a single ball and other balls are blocking orthodox use of cushions (see diagram 96). The technique of swerving the cue-ball involves raising the butt of the cue and striking a sharp glancing blow at the left-hand side of the cue-ball (or right-hand side, as the case may be). The ordinary effect of using side (i.e. the cue-ball pushing out to the right before spinning to the left) will be exaggerated both by the downward angle at which the cue meets the cue-ball and by the tip going across the cue-ball rather than through it. Aim just to miss the intervening ball and, as it passes it, the 'second-phase' spin should start to operate and swerve the cue-ball to the right.

The final position of all the balls is even more difficult to predict with a swerve shot than with other escapes, but, with any luck at all, the cue-ball and the object-ball should at least finish some distance apart.

One final point about snookering: watch the scoreboard! If you are, for example, 32 behind on the yellow (i.e. with only 27 'potting' points left on the table) then you need two snookers to win. However, if you pot yellow, green and brown, this makes you 23 behind, with only 18 on the table. You thus need only one snooker to draw, because the minimum penalty on the table is now 5. Much depends on the precise position of the balls, but in diagram 97 you should take yellow, green and brown, as shown, and then manoeuvre the cue-ball into position to leave a very nasty snooker behind the black. Your opponent may by now be a little nervous and he can no longer afford to miss the blue. You have already taken three of the six balls you need to keep in the game.

Leading on from this, it is a common mistake, as soon as your opponent needs two snookers or even one, to start trickling balls over the pocket – the theory being that if you make your opponent pot all the remaining balls he cannot win. If only the pink and black remain, this argument is flawless, but, if a number of colours remain, what generally happens is that your opponent accepts the free gifts and then *snookers* you. Do not forget that, if your opponent needs snookers, he not only has to get the snookers (and you have to miss them) but he must also pot *all* the balls. Do not do half the job for him!

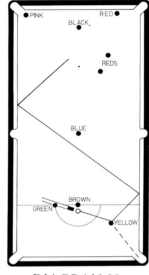

DIAGRAM 98

Another common mistake when a player fails to escape from a snooker and leaves another snookered position is for his opponent to ask him to play again. Sometimes this is a sound enough decision but, as in diagram 98, it is a mistake to make this decision too hastily. It is true that this snooker is a very nasty one but, even so, it would still be better to exercise your option to take a free ball. Nominate yellow as your free ball and screw up the table for the pink. There are several reds open in the top part of the table and you should, therefore, finish the game with a useful break. If, on the other hand, you were to ask your opponent to play again, he could possibly leave you safe (even if he gives another 4 away) and you might not have such a good opening again. *When there is a reasonable chance, always attack.*

Snooker: Doubles, Sets, Plants and Hints on Match Play

This last chapter is something of a miscellany, covering certain situations which do not fall within categories covered in previous chapters and also offering a few general hints on how to approach a match, whether it is in the Amateur Championship, local league match or humble club handicap.

DOUBLES

Diagram 99 shows five positions in which it is possible either to start or to continue a break by means of a double. This entails playing the object-ball into a cushion at such an angle that it will rebound into a pocket. Shot 1 is one of the easiest doubles on the table, since the object-ball is near enough the middle pocket to provide a reference point for the opposite middle pocket, into which you hope the object-ball will rebound.

Most professionals and good amateurs would be successful with shot 1 nine times out of ten for the half-ball angle is easy to assess. So too is the full-ball contact in shot 2, where the path of the cue-ball to the object-ball and of the object-ball from the cushion to the middle pocket makes a perfect V

Double angles are much more difficult to assess if the object-ball is further away from the middle pocket and even more so if the angle at which the cue-ball must strike the object-ball is not immediately obvious. For instance, in shot 5, the object-ball is a little way off the side cushion, so the drill is to work out the cue-ball/object-ball contact, which will put the object-ball on the V-shaped line necessary to complete the double. This looks easy

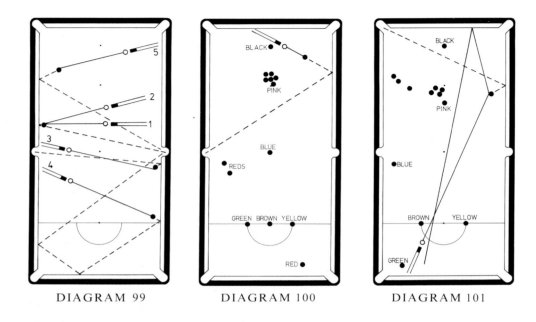

DIAGRAM 99   DIAGRAM 100   DIAGRAM 101

enough on the diagram but, in practice, selecting the exact spot which the object-ball should strike on a long length of cushion is very difficult.

This leads on to a good general rule to adopt in almost any double you play, namely: do not attempt a double unless it is likely that the cue-ball will run into a safe position.

Shot 3 in this diagram, a species known as a cut-back double, often offers a chance of safety, coupled with the pot, since the cue-ball, in going across the object-ball to make the correct doubling contact, will then run down towards the baulk cushion.

Doubles in which the object-ball enters a corner pocket after striking a side cushion are more difficult to gauge than middle pocket doubles and in most cases such doubles represent a greater risk, since the cue-ball tends to remain somewhere in the middle of the table. If this is so, there cannot be more than 6′ or 7′ between the cue-ball and the object-ball for your opponent's next shot, a distance (or lack of it) which puts the odds in your opponent's favour.

Often, a preferable alternative to the corner-pocket double is the cocked-hat double shown in shot 4. Here, the object-ball is sent off the baulk and side cushions to enter the middle pocket, while the cue-ball, struck above centre, will run through, so that it finishes somewhere near the baulk cushion. This is not as difficult as it looks, because the assessment of the angle depends on your being able to visualise the object-ball completing three sides of a rectangle (as shown) with part of the side cushion acting as the fourth side.

Some of the shots in diagram 99 strongly imply that doubles can be played as 'shots to nothing', but diagrams 100 and 101 make this more explicit. In diagram 100, the safety shot from the pack of reds down the table towards the baulk cushion is not going to put your opponent in trouble and indeed it may well give him an opening, because some reds are in the bottom half of the table. Therefore, the shot you should play here is to double the red as shown. If successful, you will have a good position on the black; if unsuccessful, there will be nothing left for your opponent, even though you would not actually have him in trouble.

In diagram 101, however, it is possible to combine an attempt at a double with a really aggressive safety stroke. This cross double, so called because the cue-ball goes across the object-ball, doubles a red towards (and hopefully into) the corner pocket, while the cue-ball bounces off the top cushion to return somewhere near the baulk cushion. If the red goes in, the green will be available to continue the break; if it does not, your opponent will have a tricky safety shot.

SETS AND PLANTS

Sets and plants can occur at any time in a frame but they most frequently occur when there is a cluster of reds between the pink and black spots.

A set occurs when two object-balls are touching in such a way that, when contacted by the cue-ball at almost any angle, the second object-ball will be potted. One must emphasize *almost any angle*, because a very thin contact creates something akin to a squeeze effect, which leads the second object-ball to miss the pocket by a couple of inches. Usually, the most difficult element in this shot is overcome merely by recognising that the

83

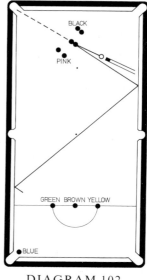

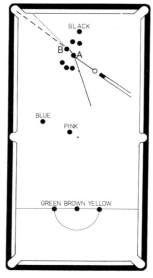

DIAGRAM 102   DIAGRAM 103

set is there – something which is not always obvious when there are many balls clustered nearby.

As with an ordinary pot, you should not be content simply with potting the second object-ball; play for position to continue the break. If you are playing a screw back (as in diagram 102) bear in mind that the cue-ball is, in effect, striking an object-ball which is twice as heavy, as the two reds offer twice as much resistance to the initial impact of the object-ball than is ordinarily the case with one red. This means that it is possible to screw back much further with less effort.

Diagram 103 shows an example of a plant, a type of shot generally more difficult than a set, because the two object-balls are not touching and thus have to strike each other at a particular angle for the pot to be completed. The best way of assessing these angles is to imagine for the moment that the first object-ball is, in fact, the cue-ball. For example, shape up to red A in diagram 103 as if it were the cue-ball and thus assess the fact that you will need a three-quarter ball contact on red B to pot it. Continue an imaginary line through that point of contact towards the cushion and

84

try to memorise the point at which red A would strike the cushion if red B were not in the way. You will need to bring your utmost concentration to bear on this when you return to the cue-ball and aim at red A. As with a set, play position from your attempted plant, in this case screwing back to take the blue in the middle pocket.

Years of practice and experience are necessary to become really proficient at plants, but even good players do not have a very high success rate with (and therefore do not often attempt) plants which involve anything below a half-ball contact. This is because the difficulty of gauging this type of shot is compounded if both object-balls and the pocket cannot be kept more or less squarely in your main line of vision.

HINTS ON MATCH PLAY

Even if you have thoroughly absorbed the entire contents of this book, there will be many things that you will find out only through playing a great deal on all sorts of tables against a wide variety of opponents. Meanwhile, here are a few hints on how to make the best of what skill you have acquired in any competitive matches you may play.

First, assuming that you have long since fulfilled the minimum requirement of buying one cue and keeping to it, make sure that you maintain it in the best possible condition. Keep it in a cue case, of course, and be careful not to leave it somewhere exceptionally warm (e.g. leaning up against a radiator) or exceptionally cold (e.g. overnight in the middle of winter in the back of a car). In either case, the cue will probably warp.

Once you have made sure that you have a tip which is neither rock hard nor spongey, check that it is domed, so that its roundness grips the shape of the ball, something that is impossible with a flat tip.

Constant chalking (most top players chalk their cue every two or three shots) can lead to a build up of chalk on the tip, which needs to be broken up by pressing a file into it in order to leave a slightly abrasive surface. If you do not do this, a shiny surface is gradually created and miscues tend to become more frequent.

Always carry your own block of chalk with you because a cue tip does not take kindly to having several different varieties applied to it in quick succession. Use chalk which stays on the tip and does not fly off in great clouds when the tip strikes the cue-ball.

On the evening of a match, always leave yourself enough time to reach the appointed venue without having to make a last minute dash. There is nothing worse than having to start a match a minute or so after reaching a club, without giving yourself chance to compose yourself.

Do not eat a big meal before you play. A heavy meal tends to dull the senses and, once your nerves start to play up in the middle of a match, you may start to feel uncomfortable. This in itself is a distraction you cannot afford.

Try to approach each match, at whatever level, with the idea that you are going to play your very best in relation to the positions which may come your way. A tournament golfer is, in a sense, competing against other golfers but, in essence, he is competing against the course, trying to get round in the least number of shots. This should be your philosophy, in that you should concentrate less on what your opponent is doing than what you yourself are doing. This is of course easier said than done, but it will certainly be to your advantage, particularly when things are tense, to concentrate on seeing the shot as it really is without letting thoughts of its consequences intrude. As soon as you start to think 'I've only got to pot yellow and green and he can't win', you are dissipating your concentration on the shot in hand. These thoughts are inevitable, but the trick is to get rid of them before you actually settle down to play the shot.

Similarly, if you start to play a pot with two or three ideas in your mind about what you are attempting to do positionally, there is every chance that the pot will be missed. Clarity of thought before you actually get down to play the shot is essential. If you find yourself down on a shot and are still uncertain about what you are trying to do, you should get up, chalk your cue and consider the matter until your intentions are clear.

Above all, enjoy the game. Enjoy the close matches as well as the easy ones. Learn from your mistakes if you can and try to analyse how good players approach individual situations.

General Glossary

Break	A sequence of scoring shots.
Check side	Spin which narrows the angle the cue-ball takes from the cushion.
Cue-ball	The ball struck with the cue.
'D'	The semi-circle (radius $11\frac{1}{2}''$) which is inscribed on the baulk line and from which all strokes must be made when the striker is in hand.
Forcing shot	Any shot considerably above medium pace.
Full-ball shot	A contact in which the cue-tip, the centre of the cue-ball and the centre of the object-ball form a straight line.
Half-ball shot	A contact in which half the cue-ball covers half the object-ball at the moment of impact.
In hand	The situation wherein a player, having scored an in-off (at billiards), can place the cue-ball by hand in the 'D' for his next shot. In snooker, when one's opponent has gone in-off, the next shot is played from the 'D'.
In-off	When the cue-ball enters a pocket after contacting another ball. In snooker, any shot which ends with the cue-ball in the pocket is described as an in-off, whether an object-ball is involved or not.
Kiss	A second contact on the object-ball.
Natural angle	Any angle which the cue-ball may take after striking an object-ball at medium pace without side or screw.
Running side	Spin which widens the angle that the cue-ball takes from a cushion.
Safe position	When the balls are so situated that a scoring stroke looks unlikely.
Safety shot	A shot in which a player makes no attempt to score, but intends to leave his opponent unable to score.
Screw	Backspin.
Side	Sidespin.
Stun	A shot in which the cue-ball is stopped dead (straight shot) or a shot in which the cue-ball is struck slightly below centre to widen the angle it takes from the object-ball (angled shot).

Billiards Glossary

Anchor cannon
The method of scoring by which the two object-balls are suspended on the upper and lower jaws of a corner pocket so that an infinite number of consecutive cannons can be made.

Baulk
The area of the table behind the line (baulk line) marked 29″ from the bottom cushion.

Cannon
The scoring stroke in which the cue-ball contacts both object-balls (value 2 points).

Close cannon
A cannon in which all three balls start and finish in close proximity.

Coup
Striking the cue-ball into a pocket without contacting another ball.

Hazard
A pot, an in-off, or a combination of the two.

Long loser
An in-off played into a top pocket when the cue-ball is in hand.

Miss
Failure to strike either object-ball.

Pot
Propelling the cue-ball on to an object-ball to send the latter into a pocket.

Stringing
A practice sometimes adopted to decide which player shall begin the game or have the choice of ball. Each player plays a white from the baulk line to the top cushion to bring it back as near as possible to the baulk cushion. The player whose ball finishes nearest the baulk cushion has the choice.

Swing
When the cue-ball follows a wide arc after contacting an object-ball at about half-ball with considerable force; a shot usually employed to widen the angle taken by the cue-ball to achieve an in-off or a cannon.

Snooker Glossary

Break-off	The first shot of a frame in which the striker plays at the unbroken triangle of reds.
Clear the table	A sequence of shots in which a player pots all the balls left on the table.
Double	A shot by which an object-ball enters a pocket after striking one or more cushions.
Free ball	If a player is snookered after a foul shot by his opponent, he may nominate any coloured ball as a red. If it is potted, he scores 1 and can then nominate a colour in the usual way. If all the reds have left the table, the free ball is nominated (valued at the same number of points as the lowest value ball on the table) and the colours are then taken in sequence. N.B.: for the purposes of this rule a player is deemed to be snookered if he cannot hit both extremities of the object-ball.
Maximum break	A sequence of shots in which a player takes all fifteen reds, fifteen blacks and all the colours to score 147.
Plant	A position in which the first object-ball is played on to a second object-ball in such a way as to make the second object-ball enter a pocket.
Set	A position in which two object-balls are touching in such a way that the second ball is certain to be potted however the first object-ball is struck.
Shot to nothing	A position in which a player attempts to pot in such a way as to leave himself in position to continue his break if successful, but will leave the cue-ball in a safe position for his opponent if unsuccessful.
Snooker	A position in which the cue-ball cannot hit an object-ball because of an intervening ball.

Useful Addresses

The full rules of Billiards and Snooker are available from: Billiards and Snooker Control Council, Alexandra Chambers, 32 John William Street, Huddersfield. This body also organises the English domestic amateur game.

OTHER GOVERNING BODIES

AUSTRALIA   Mrs P. Poirrier, 12 Burdon Street, Keperra 4054, Queensland

CANADA   P. McNichols, 1407 Cowling Avenue, Ottawa, Ontario

GHANA   Prof. N. A. Cotei, University of Science and Technology, Kumasi

INDIA   R. K. Vissanji, 9 Wallace Street, Fort, Bombay 1

KENYA   F. Murugu, PO Box 1, Uplands

MALTA   J. Muscat, Ophir House, Adelaide Cini, Hamrun

NEW ZEALAND   B. J. Bennett, PO Box 603, New Plymouth

NORTHERN IRELAND   R. C. Lowe, 10 Linden Walk, Dunmurray, Belfast

PAKISTAN   Dr S. A. Rashid, 8 Embassy Village, G28-29, Kahkastan, Clifton, Karachi

REPUBLIC OF IRELAND   D. Dalton, 3 Field Avenue, Walkinstown, Dublin 12

SCOTLAND   J. Wallace, 14 Stenhouse Grove, Edinburgh

SOUTH AFRICA   M. Payne, 4 Laurier Close, Claremont, 7700

WALES   P. Walters, Garfield, Elm Grove, Aberdare, Glamorgan

WORLD PROFESSIONAL BILLIARDS AND SNOOKER ASSOCIATION
S. M. Green, 77 Charlemont Road, West Bromwich, West Midlands, England

Snooker Scene – The game's official magazine, Cavalier House, 202 Hagley Road, Edgbaston, Birmingham B16 9PQ